SMOKIN' HOT IN THE SOUTH

ALSO BY MELISSA COOKSTON

*Smokin' in the Boys' Room: Southern Recipes
from the Winningest Woman in Barbecue*

SMOKIN' HOT IN THE SOUTH

New Grilling Recipes from the
Winningest Woman in Barbecue

MELISSA COOKSTON

Andrews McMeel
Publishing®

a division of Andrews McMeel Universal

Jalapeño Bacon–Wrapped Scallops with Blood Orange Glaze (page 133)

CONTENTS

CHAPTER 1
The Pitmaster's Basics · 1

CHAPTER 2
Rubs, Seasonings, and Sauces · 15

CHAPTER 6
Poultry · 105

CHAPTER 7
Seafood · 123

CHAPTER 8
Star of the Show Sides and Whatnot · 137

CHAPTER 9
Desserts · 155

Grilled Asian Pork Tenderloin with Watermelon Rind Pickles and Minted Watermelon Salad (page 58)

INTRODUCTION

JUST MAKE IT TASTE GOOD

I am an unabashed, dyed-in-the-wool, ever-lovin' Southern girl. The South, most particularly the Mississippi Delta region, has shaped my thoughts and my style in life, leading me to take time to enjoy but with a fierce competitive spirit. The South is about contrasts—a slow Southern drawl coupled with an exceedingly sharp wit, people who toil every day but still take time to enjoy a sunset, an appreciation of tradition but a great enjoyment of the modern, and food that appears simple but explodes with flavor.

Frankly, it's an eclectic mix.

Southern food is much more than "soul food" and biscuits (not that I will ever complain about a well-made biscuit). Our chefs bring out the best of natural goodness around them, because many of them have a great appreciation of it. I was taught to value the bounty of the land and appreciate the work of others. Our culinary traditions do the same—they sprang from necessity coupled with imagination. Take the leftovers, the inexpensive, the plentiful, and the everyday and combine them with cooking methods and seasonings that leave the palate happy and the soul fulfilled.

In this book, I want to share the joy I get in grilling and smoking some of my favorite recipes. At home I am a "Let's change this up a little" type of cook and am always trying to find a way to inject new twists into old traditions. Much of this comes from using some of the South's indigenous ingredients and signature culinary items and shaking them up with different flavors and spices, such as charring fresh okra to give it a unique texture and flavor. Some of it comes from cooking dishes, normally made inside a kitchen, outdoors, like my Caramelized Fig Clafoutis (page 158). If you've been through a summer in the South, you'll understand why you try to keep the heat out of the kitchen, but the main focus is on creating something special and unique.

Food is very personal. Nothing will illustrate this more than the humble side dish coleslaw. When I was working on my restaurants' (Memphis Barbecue Company) recipes, I had to make a dish that would not only stand on its own but also complement a pulled-pork sandwich, which regional tradition dictates that we serve topped with slaw. There are other factors I have to consider for every restaurant recipe, such as ease of preparation and consistency, but the main focus points are how will it be served and what will it be served with. However, people in the South like slaw (or potato salad) the way their mother made it. The problem is that I don't know their mother or how she made her coleslaw, although I understand their issue. Sometimes it's hard to stray from your personal culinary traditions, but that's one reason I love cooking the way I do—a bit of tradition, a bit of new, and some smoke and fire to help wrap it together. In this book, as an example, my Grilled Lime-Cilantro Slaw (page 85) is certainly not like your mother's, and it brings a fresh take to a common dish.

I've been very lucky; I have managed to take a passion and make it a career. I've managed to live on the edge and compete in barbecue contests as a living (something I absolutely do NOT recommend) and build that into a string of World BBQ Championships and successful restaurants. My passion for great barbecue has quite naturally led me to explore my Southern culinary heritage more fully, and I

have had many rich experiences because of it. In the same breath, I will tell you I also don't like to be constrained and bound by certain ingredients, flavors, or ideas of what someone thinks is mandatory. Someone once asked me what was important for flavor on the barbecue circuit, and my answer to him was the same as my answer to anyone who asked about making dinner: "Just make it taste good." Good food transcends any preconceived notions about regional flavors, food "rules," cooking procedures, or anything else. Just try it; you may like it!

SMOKE AND FIRE

I absolutely love cooking with fire. Sometimes I use fire as a slow and gentle companion, gently basting meats with smoke and heat. Sometimes it should be a roaring inferno, reddening your face as it crackles while caramelizing the crust on a beautiful steak. At all times it should be in your control. That's what this book is about—using fire in all its forms to create beautiful, Southern-influenced food imbued with soul.

The culinary traditions of the South have greatly expanded in the last few years. Long a bastion of long-simmered vegetables and deep-fried anything, we have grown to love the influences of southwestern flavors, Asian spices, and the flavor palate of the French (well, we had to fix that a little). In this book we will take a simple grill and use it to fire-roast homegrown green tomatoes for a fiery take on a pizza sauce and use the barbecue smoker to lovingly add a Southern influence to porchetta. I must admit a definite bias toward the beautifully Latin-influenced foods of the Southwest and love how roasting and smoking can tame some chiles from raging infernos to gentle signal fires. Dishes like Grilled Duck Breast and Collard Greens with Bacon (page 116) offer a new take on what are essentially Deep South staples. This book is

about cooking outside on your grill or smoker, and, yes, although I do occasionally revert to a "tried and true" Southern cooking method, I believe there are very few items that can't be improved with the addition of some smoke or fire.

In my first book, *Smokin' in the Boys' Room*, I went through my competition barbecue recipes, cooking procedures, and standard barbecue items. While there will be some similar territory in this book, it will be more focused on using fresher flavors, more herbs, and the different seasoning components in Southern-based cooking. Grilling or barbecuing doesn't have to be a long, drawn-out affair, although you can achieve some sublime results when you put in the time. Most of these recipes are easily prepared and cooked on a variety of grills, of which I have quite the assortment.

The purpose of this book is to allow you to create great dishes, sometimes built on tradition, sometimes out of your comfort zone, by removing the intimidation factor. Try it; you can do it! We have a saying in my house when I'm experimenting and when something doesn't come out the way I envision: "There's always pizza!" However, when things really work, when that dish just comes together, when it's even better than you envisioned, you get a great sense of self-fulfillment from bringing something new and unique to the table. No recipe in this book is incredibly difficult. No dish will require a two-day braise just to get a base sauce to start the dish, and nothing should take you too far out of your culinary comfort zone, but I do want you to press the edges just a bit. Push the boundaries of what is "normal"; you just might find a creativity that you never knew you had.

CHAPTER 1

THE PITMASTER'S BASICS

When I was growing up, I heard the term "land poor" bandied around to describe a family that had the majority of its wealth tied up in landholdings, typically farmland. Since I was attacked by the barbecue bug, I've had many times where I have been "cooker poor." Back when I literally made my living on the barbecue competition circuit, our smokers were a huge investment for my family, in both money and time. Many times my smokers (and how well I used them) have been the difference between eating tuna fish sandwiches and eating a steak.

This is absolutely not to say that you must invest thousands of dollars in a smoker or a grill, although it is easy to be romanced by one of the high-dollar units available today. You have to take a step back and evaluate your needs, your budget, and ease of use of the many different types. There is absolutely no perfect grill or smoker available. Each type has its pros and cons and needs to be looked at in that light. In this book, I am going to use a variety of smokers and grills to show the versatility of some as well as explain how to adapt certain smokers to achieve desired results.

GRILLS, COOKERS, AND SMOKERS

I could really write an entire book on the different grills, cookers, and smokers available today, and I probably still wouldn't cover all the possible selections. So I'm going to take the easy road and just talk here about the types that I use.

Gas Grills: I've stated before that I'm not quite the purist when it comes to barbecuing and grilling as some people in the industry. I believe that if it makes you happy, then it's OK! Who am I to tell people their belief in what makes great barbecue is wrong, although I do reserve the right to correct someone for misusing the terms *barbecue* and *grilling*; they are NOT interchangeable! Gas grills are convenient and, if used properly, can produce great food. Also, I love rotisserie cooking—there is something wonderful about trussing up a whole chicken on a spit and roasting it.

Charcoal Grills: Even though it is so convenient to hit that button on a gas grill and start cooking, charcoal grills are probably the most common form of grill available today—and with good reason. They're usually less expensive than the other types, versatile, and they produce a great flavor when used appropriately. The lower-end models are fine for any type of grilling. They can even be set up for smoking by using an indirect cooking method, where all the fuel is put on one side of the grill and the meat on the other, preferably with a water pan under or beside the meat to help with temperature control and moisture. Larger, more expensive models are usually made with heavier-gauge metal, a tighter build to control airflow, and better grates.

Ceramic Cookers: These types of grills, most notably the Big Green Egg (the XL model happens to grace my patio and is used quite often), are very versatile cookers and should be at least a contender for everyone's backyard. By slightly changing the air intakes, exhaust, and fuel, one can easily smoke at a low and slow rate, turn it into a searing-hot grill, or even create a brick-oven-style pizza oven. For home use, I highly recommend them as they are about the most versatile cooker available. Go to Biggreenegg.com for more information.

Gas Grill

Charcoal Grill

Ceramic Cooker

Smoker

Smokers: The evolution of the smoker paralleled the rise in competition barbecue. The ubiquitous "barrel grill" made from a prefabricated piece of pipe or propane tank has morphed into double-insulated high-tech pieces of equipment with built in water pans (or not) and reverse flow with convection fans. I learned to cook on a barrel grill that was so drafty I had to position it just right to get it to temperature, which it could hold for approximately 3 minutes before I had to stoke or reposition it. However, at the end of the day the cooker doesn't matter; it's the cook. Now, that being said, I have graduated to some fancier smokers, but they are definitely not a necessity outside of the world of competition barbecue unless you are intent on winning the backyard barbecue wars. While there are several great smoker companies out there today, I use Pitmaker (pitmaker.com) pits on my demonstration trailer, which is also what I use to cook in the Kansas City Barbeque Society contests. These guys build nothing but quality products, and the pride George and Victor take in building their pits shows in their work.

Wet Versus Dry Smokers: On the circuit I continually hear people tout the advantages of their favorite types of smoker, whether it's a water smoker or a dry-heat smoker (and generally they will throw in an insult about the opposing type just for fun). Frankly, both camps are correct as both smokers can produce absolutely succulent cuisine. I won my world championships on water smokers (really big water smokers for cooking whole hogs!) and use them frequently today. They have some key attributes such as moisture and temperature consistency that make them great choices. Conversely, I prefer some meats cooked on a dry cooker, and many world championships have been won on them as well. This really comes down to a personal preference; don't let anybody tell you otherwise.

TOOLS YOU ABSOLUTELY NEED TO GET

Charcoal Starting Tool(s): Why people still use lighter fluid is beyond me. If you are one that practices this, know that you have been properly chastised and pledge that you will never again subject your family and friends to the taste of lighter fluid in their dinner. There are many different types of charcoal starters to use that will not leave any taste in your food. I generally use a charcoal chimney when I'm starting my larger smokers, as it will light a large amount of charcoal at once. There are also electric starters, all-natural fire-starter briquettes (typically compressed sawdust), and wax starters. All are good and will leave you with a fine start to your fire without the bad aftertastes.

Fat Separator Cup: This helps separate the beefy or porky goodness from rendered fats. In a pinch, use a plastic drink bottle with a cap, pour in the rendered beef or pork

juices, and turn upside down (after putting on the cap!). After the fat rises to the top, you can pour out the good stuff for use in a sauce.

Good Knives: Having good knives does not mean having the most expensive knives, but it certainly excludes the cheapest. I bought knives piecemeal at first and built up my set over time. Generally, one can do just about anything with a 6 or 8-inch chef's knife and/or santoku (my favorite), a 10 or 12-inch slicer, a 3-inch paring knife, and a 6-inch fillet knife or utility knife. Handle the knives before purchasing, as brands will feel different due to the weight of the blade, bolster, and handle. A good knife will feel like an extension of your hand. Keep them sharp and they will reward you with years of service.

Cheap Cotton Gloves: These are "hot gloves" that I wear underneath my nitrile gloves. They allow me to handle hot meats for long periods of time and maintain some degree of touch so I can test the texture of the meat. You can get the fancy, silicone mitts or gloves if you want, but I have always preferred these when handling meat.

Injectors: Ninety percent of the time I use simple, cheap plastic injection needles when I am injecting meat. You can get larger, pump-style injectors, but unless you are moving into cooking whole hogs or a large quantity of meat, there's no need, and many times these larger injectors will negatively impact the meat as they are too forceful.

Insulated Coolers or Cambro: A Cambro is a brand of insulated boxes built to hold sheet pans and metal pans for the restaurant and catering industry. Barbecue folks use them for resting briskets, butts, and ribs for extended periods of time as they hold heat extremely well. A normal cooler will suffice for holding meat; just don't try to rest a brisket in with your cold drinks.

Immersion Blender and/or Food Processor/Blender: These make short work of vinaigrettes, marinades, sauces, and other emulsions and purées. Plus, they're fun to use.

Thermometers/Biotherms: A good-quality, fast-reading meat thermometer is essential to producing perfect food, especially for someone who is not a professional cook. Fast-cooking items or meats that need to be cooked past a danger zone, such as chicken, require the use of a thermometer more than longer-cooking items. The notable brand used on the barbecue circuit is Thermapen (available at thermoworks.com, where their "super fast, splash proof Thermapen" is the utensil of choice), and many an argument has been waged on which color is "fastest" (correct answer: they're all the same speed). There are other brands available that will do just as well, including simple stick thermometers. Always calibrate your thermometer using boiling water (adjusting for altitude if necessary). I also use the probes to test for tenderness in addition to temperature.

Oven Thermometer: A thermometer that reads the internal temperature of meat while it's cooking on the grill, in the smoker, or in the oven allows you to get a sense of where the meat is during the cooking process while keeping the door closed. If you're looking, you ain't cooking! Many pitminders will also have a built-in probe for reading the internal temperature as well as the pit temperature.

Map to the Local Farmers' Market: I always try to support local businesses, craftsmen, and farmers by frequenting farmers' markets to get locally sourced products, as well

as help craft farmers. However, buyer beware, as I have noticed more and more people purchasing products through a restaurant supply company and just reselling it (generally produce). Look around for the boxes used to bring their products in. If they are stamped with a brand or another company, that product probably wasn't grown by that vendor. Farmers' markets are great sources for humanely raised meats as well as produce and seasonings, and often have a local vendor or two selling some great barbecue. What could be better?

Spice Grinder/Mortar and Pestle: A clean coffee grinder works great as a spice grinder and is fairly inexpensive. For small amounts, I find a mortar and pestle works just as well, plus I can get the spice ground to the exact consistency I want.

Grill Baskets: I keep several sizes of grill baskets at the house and use them often. Generally if I think I can cook something without using one I always will, as this eliminates one more item to clean. However, some foods such as vegetables or fish may benefit from a grill basket as you can more easily move it to different heat zones without losing it through the grates or tearing it apart.

Grill Brushes, Tongs, Some Old Towels, and Some Elbow Grease: I cannot tell you how many times at a barbecue contest I have seen people pull up with dirty, foul-smelling barbecue smokers and start cooking. It's not "seasoned"; it's filthy. Clean your grills! I once lost a contest because the team next to mine had such a malodorous scent that when one judge visited my booth, they thought it was my area and marked me down. An old adage in the restaurant business is "People eat with their eyes." This means beautifully prepared and plated foods will whet people's appetite. While I fully believe this is true, I also believe we "taste with the nose." Much of the "flavor" we pick up from foods comes from the aroma and the way our sense of smell integrates with our sense of taste. Great-smelling food will absolutely taste better; bad aromas will necessarily dull or negate good flavors. My grill grates are cleaned before and after every cook. My smokers are fully cleaned after every cook, especially before a barbecue contest.

"Seasoning" a smoker is much like seasoning a cast-iron skillet. Allowing oil to bond to the metal through heat will keep it rust free and nonstick. However, don't use that as an excuse not to clean it! After cleaning and allowing the smoker to dry, spray it with a good coating of spray oil and it will remain rust free.

Proper grilling requires a clean, heated grate. Always oil your grates before placing your food on them, using an old towel and a small container of a high-heat-threshold oil, such as peanut oil. Using tongs, dip the towel in the oil and lightly brush the grates. This will help keep foods from sticking and forming a buildup on your grates but also will aid in getting professional-looking grill marks.

TOOLS YOU WILL WONDER HOW YOU EVER DID WITHOUT

Membership in a Restaurant Supply Store: In many larger cities, there are large, warehouse-style stores that carry restaurant equipment and/or food. Generally equipment and supplies made for restaurants are going to stand up to wear and tear significantly better than products you can purchase at most retail stores. Many also tend to offer hard-to-find spices or foods at a much more reasonable price than your normal grocery store.

Chamber Vacuum: This is one of those expensive, takes-up-lots-of-space pieces of equipment that you think you will never get good value out of having. However, it has become integral in my kitchen. If you want to make a foray into sous-vide cooking, it is a great tool. I use this for quite a few things, such as vacuum sealing meats for the freezer, packaging trimmed meats to take to a contest, compressing and flavorizing fruit, quickly marinating meats (what may take overnight otherwise gets done in 30 minutes), quick pickling, and sealing items such as leftover sauces and freezing them. It's worth the cost alone just to compress watermelon. Truly awesome and fun to use.

Meat Maximizer: This is a forty-five-blade meat tenderizer with spring-loaded action, commonly called in the restaurant industry a "Jaccard" after a leading manufacturer. However, there are many, less expensive brands available at most kitchen stores. You use this tool by pressing the maximizer along the surface of the meat so the blades cut through the meat. As the incisions are very small, they are not noticeable, especially after cooking.

This takes the place of using a huge meat tenderizer, flailing away at a poor piece of meat and beating it into an unrecognizable pulp. It's great for helping "push" seasonings into the meat as well, and I use it mainly for this purpose.

Baking Stone: Used in a grill setting, these allow you to get true "brick-oven" flavors and are easy to use and clean. They can be cumbersome to move around and store, but the results make it worthwhile. I have several sizes that can be used on multiple grills.

Pitminders or Controlled Draft Systems: These are electronic thermostats that operate a fan to help a smoker or a grill achieve and maintain a certain temperature. Generally they are much more suited for use in smokers, but certain grills, such as a Big Green Egg, respond very well to them. Keep in mind that for a pitminder to be effective, you must have a tightly built grill where you can limit the air intake for the fire to the pitminder fan. If you can do that, a pitminder will help control

your temperatures. You still must use good fire-building techniques and control the amount of fuel for them to be effective. I use mine as a babysitter for a few minutes, not as a substitute for running my pits. Another very important note: take grill temperatures from where your items are cooking, not where the temperature gauge is located. A pit may be 350°F in the middle of the cooking chamber, but only 220°F at the grate level. Keep this in mind when cooking any recipe.

THE ART OF THE FIRE

Building a fire is an art unto itself. In a grill situation, where the cooking time is necessarily shortened, the requisite skills aren't as important as the end result. Generally speaking, get the grill hot enough to properly cook your food and you'll be OK. It may not be efficient, you may be burning twice as much fuel as necessary, or that grill may keep burning long into the night after everyone is in bed, but you can get the job done. However, when you want to undertake true barbecue, proper fire building becomes much more important. The food will be exposed to the results of your fire for much longer, so a poorly built fire can easily detract from the flavors of the meat. Also, if the fire is not built correctly, you expend significantly more time, energy and frustration trying to fix it during the cooking process.

CHARCOALS AND WOODS

Charcoal comes in two main forms, lump and briquettes. Lump charcoal is made of whole pieces of wood that have been exposed to heat in a low-oxygen environment. This smolders the wood and leaves just the carbon. Briquettes are usually made from sawdust exposed to a similar process, then ground and formed into a briquette, along with certain binders to help keep its form. Lump charcoal tends to be all-natural (although I have found plenty of rocks, nails, and the like in bags) while briquettes normally contain additives. Lump charcoal burns hotter and produces less ash, while briquettes burn more consistently and leave you with more to clean up. Lump charcoal, depending on the brand, can help flavor your meat, while briquettes usually impart a neutral or no flavor. Lump charcoal needs a much "tighter" cooker to control the airflow to it and manage the heat. Briquettes, by their nature, will burn more consistently in a regular grill. For smoking, I generally start with lump charcoal and then move to briquettes during the middle and later stages.

I maintain a stockpile of different woods in my garage in both sticks and chunks. I use wood for both flavor and heat. I generally keep the following types of wood around.

Apple: Sweet, light flavor, and a lighter smoke ring.
Cherry: Full, robust flavor that produces a beautiful red smoke ring.
Peach: A stronger, more unique flavor than most fruitwood, but produces a very light smoke ring.
Oak: Neutral flavor, golden-red-hued smoke ring.
Pecan: Slightly more intense flavor than oak with a red smoke ring; one of my favorites.
Hickory: Produces a robust flavor and smoke ring but tends to overpower meats rather quickly, can make meat very dark or black, and can take on bitter overtones; I use it only as an accent wood.
Mesquite: Can be a nice wood for grilling as it burns very hot and will quickly add some flavor to meats. (Not being from Texas, I am not a fan of smoking with mesquite.)

I have tried many other woods as well. A few of my favorites are pear, persimmon, orange, and walnut, but they are not easily obtainable, so I don't stock them. In addition, several types of wood have multiple subtypes, such as post oak, white oak, red oak, etc. I listed the main ones above as they seem to be the most readily available. I don't worry about using a particular subtype of wood as much as I try to maintain the proper amount of flavor. Keeping your fire burning cleanly and adding wood chunks a few at a time will have far more bearing on how your products taste than the specific type of wood you use.

FIRE BUILDING

Many people, especially novices, think that if some smoke is good, more MUST be better. Nope! First, you must have a clean-burning fire. By this I mean that the fire should be getting enough oxygen to combust properly and have enough flow in and through the grill or smoker to exhaust properly. A smaller, hotter fire is infinitely more desirable than a larger, smoldering fire. You don't get a clean-burning fire by packing an extra bag of charcoal on the fire because it was on sale; you get it by properly igniting and *tending* the fire.

Tending a fire is becoming a lost art in the barbecue world. With the advent of insulated cookers and "pitminders" many people have gravitated to a "set it and forget it" mentality. That is fine and dandy if the weather and wind are perfect, but if you never learn to properly tend a fire on those occasions where you are "fighting your cooker," you will wish you had. Cooking in the climate-controlled zone of a kitchen, you never have to worry about a passing storm front; temperatures dropping 40 degrees; rain, humidity, and other factors. But when cooking outside, you almost always will have to deal with environmental issues that will have an impact on your

cooking. The way to overcome this problem is to make sure your fire is built and maintained properly. Keep a smaller fire burning strong. I never soak wood, unless it is chips I am adding to a foil boat to put in a grill. Soaking wood produces a slower, sooty fire and doesn't add a thing to the smoke permeation of the meat. Rather, add a few chunks at a time, allow them to combust cleanly, and add more if needed.

Exhaust maintenance is just as important. You should adjust the smokestack only if there is significant wind, which may be "pulling" the heat out of the cooker. If you are "backing up smoke" in the cooker—that is, smoke is coming out of places it shouldn't— then you need to open the exhaust more or put less fuel on the fire.

I will definitely admit I use cookers insulated so well you can set your glass of iced tea on top and not melt the ice. I like to use pitminders, water pans, instant-read thermometers, and any other tool I think will help. However, for years we didn't have any of those items and I cooked on simple, homemade smokers burning down wood into my own charcoal before putting in the grill. I have cooked contests week after week consecutively and used these fancy smokers during the week for catering. Using any smoker that much, I knew exactly what would happen when I would add three chunks of wood or just open the air intake a half inch. All that being said, I still continually fall back on the knowledge of how to build and maintain a fire. Even the best cookers are affected by torrential rains, high winds, and subfreezing temperatures.

A prime example of managing cookers in different weather conditions was at the inaugural Kingsford Invitational in 2012. This contest brought the winners of the largest and most prestigious barbecue contests of the year, including Memphis in May, the Jack Daniels Invitational, Kansas City Royal, the Houston Livestock Show, and some others. The contest used a head-to-head

judging system to determine the "best of the best." It was held in a field in Belle, Missouri, and the winds were constant and strong for the entire contest. To maintain a given temperature I had to use significantly more fuel as the wind was pulling the heat out of the cookers quickly. What most people don't realize when this happens is that you get a significant "convection effect" and the items will cook much more quickly than normal as the heat is pulled around your items. I lowered my target temperatures in the cooker slightly to accommodate this, and everything cooked beautifully. I ended up having a pretty good day as well, winning ribs, pork, and brisket and the Grand Champion of the event. I know that if I had stuck to my normal cooking time/temperature recipe, I would have severely overcooked some items and had a very mediocre showing.

While there are some that advocate using all wood in their smokers, aka "stick burners," I tend to keep a base of charcoal burning and then add wood for flavor and extra heat. The specific woods I choose for smoke are as much a tool as a flavoring component. They influence how I build my fire, add or lower heat, and how much I use to gently flavor my products. I try to use woods as an accent flavor, and it should never overpower the meat. Depending on the item and the smoker, my base fire may be either briquettes or lump charcoal, with hardwood(s) added to the fire. First, this allows me to keep a more consistent temperature as charcoal burns more steadily. Second, it allows me to flavor the product as I see fit, adding in whatever type or blend of woods that will best accentuate the product I am cooking.

Building a fire in a grill is very similar to building one in a smoker. First, it needs to be clean burning: Don't overload it with too much fuel. Direct grilling requires good airflow to achieve the temperatures for searing and cooking.

SETTING UP A GRILL

There are two main methods of setting up a charcoal or wood-fired grill for home use, the "direct" and "indirect" method. The direct method is used for straightforward grilling. When you want a burger, hot dogs, and the like, you fire up some charcoal or turn on the burners and start grilling. You have to use enough fuel to generate the heat levels you are looking to get. Place the item directly above the charcoal and cook to the desired level of doneness.

The indirect method is simply an offshoot of the direct method, in that you set all or most of your fire to one side of the grill and cook on the other side so as to have lower temperature on your items and less chance of charring. Generally, setting up a grill for indirect is more easily done on a rectangular or larger grill, but it can be done on square, circular, or even small grills. A water pan can be placed on top of the hot side of the grill. This will help blunt some of the heat from the grill, add moisture to the cooking chamber, and make your grill temps more consistent. Some people prefer to place the water pan underneath the item being cooked. This method is better if you are adding aromatics such as onions, herbs, juices, or wine to the water pan as the evaporation of the liquids will help carry some of those flavors up to the meats or vegetables. The classic indirect method is most often used when you are trying to mimic a smoker by putting meat on the cool side and wood and charcoal on the fuel side and thereby achieving lower temperatures on your meat so that you can generate the longer cooking time that some items need.

In this book, where I reference a "smoker," you can achieve the temperatures and performance I am using by setting up a grill in this manner. The downside to this is that it becomes labor intensive and frustrating to maintain the temperatures needed for a long smoke-cooking recipe. Being more interested in great-tasting food than the "purity" of the method, I am about to commit barbecue sacrilege with the following statement: Use your oven. Most professional barbecuers wrap their products in foil or place in an aluminum pan after a few hours under smoke. This allows them to maintain their color profile, limit the smoke flavor of the meat, speed up the cooking process, and not subject the meat to the temperature inconsistency that happens in the real world when cooking on a smoker. What's the difference between doing that and removing the item from the grill, placing it in a pan or wrapping in foil, and putting it in your oven to finish? The answer: not much. Now, when I'm cooking at my house I like to have a bit more bark and smoke flavor in a pork butt or brisket; I don't usually wrap them. However, the difference in flavor is a matter of degrees, not wholesale changes. There is no shame in keeping a good watch over a pork butt on a grill for three hours to infuse the meat with smoke and flavor, then removing it, wrapping it up, and placing it in the oven at the same temperature. Barbecue is about enjoying life and creating memories, and if your memories involve burned meat, unsuccessful cooks, and feeling too tired to enjoy the fruits of your labor because you've spent eight hours managing a fire every fifteen minutes, then maybe you're doing it wrong.

For most of the grilling recipes, I will reference setting up your grill for "two-zone" cooking. This is basically a hybrid of the direct and indirect methods, where you are using the majority of your fuel on one side and some of the fuel on the other to create two temperature zones. You can use this to do quite a few things. Most items, such as steak, duck breasts, or even vegetables, benefit from a Maillard reaction, which is the chemical reaction that changes the flavor of food when you brown or sear it. However, to cook to a desired level of doneness, they cannot handle being cooked at a browning/searing temperature for a long enough period without burning. This is where you use a

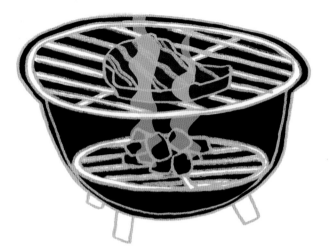

Direct Heat

Indirect Heat

two-zone cooking grid. Brown or sear the product on one side and then move it to the cooler side to finish cooking. Also, when you set a grill up in this manner, you can also use it for a variety of functions. I often will sear steaks, move them to a cooler side, then use the hot side to grill or sauté vegetables, make a sauce in a cast-iron skillet, or grill some fruit for dessert while the steak finishes.

Setting up a gas grill for your desired cooking outcome is even easier, although perhaps not as flavorful. Simply have one side on at a high temp and the other side either off or on a low setting. Adjust the heat on each side until you achieve the desired internal grill temperature. For flavor, a smoker box is an option in many gas grills, or you can wrap some wood chips in foil, poke some air holes in it, and lay near a burner to smolder. Water pans, with or without aromatics, can be used in a gas grill as well.

HEAT TABLE

These are the "rules of thumb" I use when grilling. Although I don't usually use a thermometer on a grill, this will equate temperatures to terminology I use in this book.

Searing Heat = 600+°F, used for pizza stones and quick grill marks and sears

High Heat = 500° to 600°F, used for initial searing, sautéing, and quick-grilling items

Medium-High Heat = 400° to 500°F, general cooking zone

Medium Heat = 350° to 400°F, baking on the grill, finishing items

Medium-Low Heat = 300° to 250°F, finishing off items, setting glazes

Low Heat = 250° to 300°F, longer cook time items, braising. Smoker temps normally run 225° to 300°F

I normally will check temperatures by holding my hand two to three inches above the cooking grate. On a medium-temperature grill, you can usually hold your hand there for six to seven seconds, adding or subtracting two to three seconds for every higher temperature grade. Using this method you can fairly accurately guesstimate the temperature. Most grills and smokers will have a temperature gradient where they have different heat levels on different areas of the grill. You can use this to your advantage in cooking. For example, I will place a steak on the hottest part of the grill initially to gain some quick sear and set my grill marks, then move it to a cooler part to allow the internal temperature to rise to the desired level.

Barbecuers use temperature gradients as well. Even on a well-insulated smoker, there will usually be hotter areas where the heat enters the cooking chamber. This can be used to cook different meats, speed up or slow down cooking, develop bark, etc. I use the famous "biscuit test" when trying out a new smoker to cut down on the learning curve. Simply open a can of biscuits and lay them out on various parts of the grill. Some will cook more quickly than others, showing you where the hot spots are. Many smokers with "dry cookers" will place a water pan over the main hot spot to add humidity to the cooking chamber as well as help normalize the temperatures through the grill.

THE PITMASTER'S PANTRY

I have found most aspiring pitmasters fall into two categories, both of whom can be categorized by a peek into their pantry. The first type will have somewhere between ten and twenty-five different commercially prepared barbecue seasonings, sauces, etc. They tend to concentrate on the cooking aspect as opposed to the seasoning aspect of grilling and barbecue. The second type of cook will have as many esoteric salts, herbs, sweeteners, and seasonings as you can count. These people focus on creating their own blends and flavors for seasonings, sauces, marinades, and injections. While I have no problem with the former, I have always counted myself among the latter. This results in "pantry cleanout day" about once per quarter, as I have to clean out and organize out-of-date spices, mistakes, and impulse buys.

The truth is you can make seasoning blends, sauces, and whatever else that will be just as good as or better than anything you can purchase. This does not mean that you have to have a pantry with every spice known to man. Here's a list of items that I use in this book, along with a few other items that I think are important. This is not an all-inclusive list, nor is everything on it a "must have." (Well, a few, such as salts and peppers, are.)

SPICES, AROMATICS
★ Kosher salt, table or iodized salt, sea salt, and flaked or finishing salts
★ Black peppercorns, white peppercorns, pink peppercorns, and green peppercorns in brine
★ Whole, fresh garlic bulbs: garlic cloves; minced garlic; and shallots
★ Sweet onions, white onions, red onions, and scallions (green onions)
★ Dried chiles: chipotle, ancho, chile de árbol, pasilla, and guajillo
★ Chili powders: a medium or light, a hot (generally "dark"), and paprika
★ Granulated garlic and granulated onion
★ Dried herbs, cumin seeds, coriander seeds, mustard seeds, celery seeds, and fennel seeds

★ Fresh herbs: As much as possible, I try to keep a small herb garden. Basil, sage, and rosemary are especially easy to keep alive. Tarragon, thyme, oregano, cilantro, and Italian (or flat-leaf) parsley also make very frequent appearances in my recipes.
★ Jalapeños, poblanos, red and green bell peppers

OILS, VINEGARS, AND OTHER ACIDS
★ Fresh lemons, oranges and limes (I love Meyer lemons!)
★ Extra virgin olive oil
★ Peanut oil: I call for peanut oil often, as it stands up to a grill and has a neutral flavor. Grapeseed oil, canola oil, or other high-smoke-point oils are interchangeable.
★ Balsamic vinegar: I always keep a selection of good balsamics for quickly drizzling over something or for use as a dipping oil. I also keep some less-aged ones around for use in recipes and reductions.
★ Other vinegars: red wine, white wine, cider, along with citrus champagne and flavored vinegars.

SWEETENERS
★ Turbinado sugar, white sugar, light and dark brown sugar
★ Local, single-source honey. Bees are our friends— support your local apiarist!
★ Orange blossom honey, because it's awesome on a biscuit
★ Agave syrup
★ Molasses, preferably in a can from a local sorghum mill

OTHER INGREDIENTS
★ Self-rising, all-purpose, and bread flours
★ Celery, carrots
★ Yellow, white, and blue cornmeal. Self-rising versions are optional.

★ Stone-ground grits: If you're lucky enough to acquire some from the Grit Girl, Georgeanne Ross, from Oxford, Mississippi, don't share them with anyone. Hoard them! Stone-ground grits are to the pallid, bland excuse of a white "breakfast" grit as a Ferrari is to an Edsel. There are also stone-ground grits available in most supermarkets.

★ Worcestershire sauce, ketchup, and tomato paste
★ Tamarind paste. It's easier to find than it used to be.
★ Good-quality chicken and beef paste for making into stock. Yes, I know it's better to make my own, and I do occasionally and freeze it for later use. But sometimes the hours a good-quality paste saves me is worth it.
★ BACON! Because, who wants to be without bacon?

CHAPTER 2

RUBS, SEASONINGS, AND SAUCES

If there's one thing I would like you to get from this book, it is that you don't have to follow rub, seasoning, or sauce recipes exactly. When you make a seasoning blend, don't be afraid to experiment or to accentuate your favorite ingredients to bring out certain flavors in the dishes you are making. I have always found making my own seasoning blends, especially on the barbecue circuit, truly makes me feel as though "that dish is mine." It's very easy to buy a premade barbecue seasoning for example (and if you do, I sell a very fine one!), but to do it yourself will give you significantly more pride in the finished dish.

A few hints: (1) Make small batches. If it's not good, it's a lot easier to discard a small batch and start over. (2) Write things down. (I've learned this one the hard way!) (3) Certain rubs taste better grilled, and certain rubs are made for longer cook times. As an example, one of my favorite seasonings lately is my Southwest Spice Blend (page 17). However, for longer cook times and smoking, it turns rather flat. (4) Don't be afraid to experiment. In my family it's very common for all of us to have a differently seasoned main dish (chicken breast is an easy example), and we all mix and match and determine our favorite. Disagreements are part of the fun!

Whenever possible, I buy my seasonings as seeds or dried whole and then grind as needed. Seasonings lose their potency fast, and you should go through your "spice rack" occasionally and replace as needed. I find I get a much better product at a dedicated spice store since they tend to keep bulk spices and go through them faster (and it smells great inside the store). One helpful note is to date the spices when you purchase them to give you an idea of how old they are.

Many seasonings benefit from a quick toasting before use. Cumin is a good example. When purchased in powdered form, it has a good flavor that will benefit certain recipes. However, when purchased as cumin seeds, then lightly toasted and ground with a mortar and pestle, the aroma will perfume the air and make a spice blend sing. Chili powders are best made to order as well. I find it much easier to acquire certain peppers, such as chile de árbol, in their dried form and make my own powder by using a spice grinder.

All of the seasoning blends in this book will keep their flavor for about 2 to 3 months if stored in an airtight container.

This is my Basic BBQ Rub, which was also in my first book, *Smokin' in the Boys' Room*. As I still use it quite often, either by itself or as a base for other blends, I wanted to include it here as well. This is really aimed at smoking pork for multiple hours, but I love it on just about everything. Recently I took my truck to get the oil changed, and one of the guys there said, "I put it on everything, even corn flakes." I have not tested it on breakfast cereal, but you are welcome to try!

Makes about 2¾ cups

Basic "Memphis-Style" BBQ Rub

1 cup turbinado sugar

½ cup granulated sugar

½ cup kosher salt

1 tablespoon onion powder

2 tablespoons granulated garlic

1½ teaspoons cayenne

1 teaspoon finely ground black pepper

2 teaspoons dry mustard

¼ cup mild chili powder

1 teaspoon ground cumin

¼ cup plus 2 tablespoons paprika

Place the turbinado sugar in a coffee grinder and pulse until lightly powdered. Transfer to a small mixing bowl and add the remaining ingredients. Stir until well incorporated. Store in an airtight container for up to 2 months.

This seasoning has become my favorite spice blend for grilling around the house. It has a depth of flavor but tends to bring out some unique undertones in every type of meat I use it on. Store in an airtight jar and it will keep its flavor for 2 to 3 months.

You'll get absolutely the best results by using lightly toasted whole cumin, fennel, allspice, and cloves and grinding in a spice grinder, but preground is plenty good as well.

Makes about 1½ cups

Southwest Spice Blend

2 tablespoons ground coriander

2 tablespoons ground cinnamon

2 tablespoons chipotle chile powder

2 tablespoons ground cumin

2 tablespoons ground ginger

2 tablespoons granulated garlic

2 tablespoons granulated onion

2 tablespoons kosher salt

2 tablespoons coarsely ground black pepper

1 tablespoon cayenne

1 tablespoon ground allspice

1 tablespoon ground fennel seeds

1 tablespoon ground cloves

Combine all the ingredients in a small mixing bowl and stir by hand until well incorporated. Store in an airtight container for up to 2 months.

While true "blackening" is done in a very hot skillet, I like using the same spice palette on the grill when I'm looking for a spicy crust on certain dishes, like my "Blackened" Hanger Steak with Sweet Potato Hash and Fried Egg (page 88). This seasoning blend will work for the grill, the blackening skillet, or as a spicy sprinkle on dishes like Plank-Fried Crab Cakes (page 125). If you like it even spicier, increase the cayenne pepper by a teaspoon or two!

Makes about ½ cup

Blackening Seasoning

3 tablespoons paprika

2 tablespoons granulated garlic

2 teaspoons kosher salt

1 teaspoon onion powder

1 teaspoon dried thyme

1 teaspoon coarsely ground black pepper

1 teaspoon cayenne

½ teaspoon dried oregano

1 teaspoon dark chili powder

Combine all the ingredients in a small mixing bowl and stir by hand until well incorporated. Store in an airtight container for up to 2 months.

Poultry, by its nature, has a very neutral flavor palette, and sometimes I need to bring the flavor component up, especially when it will be served in a sandwich or with other dishes that may overwhelm it. This rub adds a dash of color as well as a flavor "snap" with pink and white peppercorns and will really make turkey or chicken stand out.

Makes almost ½ cup

Pepper Poultry Rub

2 tablespoons kosher salt

1 tablespoon coarsely ground black pepper

1 teaspoon white peppercorns, crushed with a mortar and pestle

1 tablespoon pink peppercorns, lightly cracked with a mortar and pestle

1 tablespoon granulated garlic

1 teaspoon onion powder

1 teaspoon chipotle chile powder

Combine all the ingredients in a small mixing bowl and stir by hand until well incorporated. Store in an airtight container for up to 2 months.

I created this rub to season pork belly, which is very fatty and needs a bit of kick to round out the flavor. I love the coriander in this mixture. When pulsing in a spice grinder (or using a mortar and pestle), don't pulverize the cracked pepper or the coriander; just "open them up" a bit so they can add flavor and texture. I also use coarsely ground black pepper here to give full pepper coverage over the meat.

Makes about 1¼ cups

"Belly Rub"

1 tablespoon coriander seeds

1 tablespoon cracked black pepper

¼ cup kosher salt

¼ cup sea salt

¼ cup turbinado sugar

2 tablespoons paprika

2 tablespoons coarsely ground black pepper

1 tablespoon mild chili powder

1 tablespoon hot red pepper flakes

1 tablespoon ancho chile powder

Place the coriander seeds and cracked black pepper in a spice grinder and lightly pulse until slightly reduced in size but not pulverized. Transfer to a mixing bowl and add the kosher and sea salts, sugar, paprika, coarsely ground black pepper, chili powder, red pepper, and ancho chile powder. Stir until well incorporated. Store in an airtight container for up to 2 months.

Beef, in general, can carry a bit more spice through the cooking process, so I like to ramp up the flavors. The different chili powders in this rub have enough flavor to withstand long cooking times but get tamed slightly by the gentle nudging of some pecan or cherry wood. I like this for fattier cuts of beef, such as my Beef Back Ribs (page 104). It also works great as a layering rub as in my Beef Brisket Flat (page 98).

Makes about 1 cup

Cow Wow Rub

2 tablespoons paprika

2 tablespoons ancho chile powder

2 tablespoons mild chili powder

¼ cup coarsely ground black pepper

¼ cup packed light brown sugar

2 tablespoons granulated garlic

2 tablespoons kosher salt

1 teaspoon cayenne

Combine all the ingredients in a small mixing bowl and stir by hand until well incorporated. Store in an airtight container for up to 2 months.

This rub is made especially for those who like to baste or mop pork through the cooking process. It has enough flavor to stand up and maintain its pop even under repeated "mops."

Makes almost 1 cup

Moppin' Dry Rub

3 tablespoons kosher salt

2 tablespoons ancho chile powder

2 tablespoons mild chili powder

2 tablespoons granulated garlic

¼ cup turbinado sugar, lightly ground in a spice grinder

1 teaspoon dried oregano

1 tablespoon coarsely ground black pepper

Combine all the ingredients in a small mixing bowl and stir by hand until well incorporated. Store in an airtight container for up to 2 months.

I made this rub especially for Dry-Aged Prime Rib (page 91), but it really works well for chicken breasts too. However, it needs to be used in a searing or smoking manner, as the flames of a grill can sometimes burn the herbs.

Makes almost 1 cup

Fresh Herb Rub

¼ cup chopped fresh flat-leaf parsley

1 tablespoon chopped fresh oregano leaves

1 tablespoon chopped fresh thyme

¼ cup kosher salt

1 tablespoon sea salt

2 tablespoons coarsely ground black pepper

3 cloves garlic, minced

2 tablespoons extra virgin olive oil

Combine all the ingredients in a small mixing bowl and stir by hand until well incorporated. Use on the same day it's made.

Fresh Herb Rub for Dry-Aged Prime Rib (page 91)

This is my go-to seasoning blend when grilling almost anything. It is flavorful, but also neutral enough to be used on a variety of different meats.

Makes about ¾ cup

Grillin' Shake

6 tablespoons kosher salt

3 tablespoons coarsely ground black pepper

1 tablespoon onion flakes, lightly ground in a spice grinder

1 tablespoon granulated garlic

½ teaspoon crushed red pepper

1 tablespoon coriander seeds, lightly ground in a spice grinder

1 teaspoon dried thyme

Combine all the ingredients in a small mixing bowl and stir by hand until well incorporated. Store in an airtight container for up to 2 months.

This is a classic steakhouse blend for seasoning steaks, and it allows the flavors of a well-marbled steak to shine. If you don't like the zip of cracked black pepper, substitute coarsely ground black pepper.

Makes almost ¼ cup, or enough for 4 steaks

Grilled Steak Seasoning

2 tablespoons sea salt

1 tablespoon cracked black pepper

1 teaspoon granulated garlic

Combine all the ingredients in a small mixing bowl and stir by hand until well incorporated.

I use this not only as an injection before cooking but also as a dip afterward. It is used simply to add some moisture and accentuate the "beefiness" of the brisket.

Makes about 2½ cups

Brisket Injection

3 cups beef stock

½ cup Worcestershire sauce

2 tablespoons granulated garlic

2 teaspoons onion powder

In a small stockpot over medium heat, bring the beef stock, Worcestershire, garlic, and onion powder to a boil. Decrease the heat to a simmer and continue to cook until reduced by one-third. Cool and store in an airtight container in the refrigerator for up to 5 days.

This is for those fans of basting and mopping through the cooking process. It works great on my Mopped Baby Back Ribs (page 74), but if you are cooking pork shoulders, butts, or spareribs and prefer to mop, it will bring out some traditional pork flavor in those as well.

Makes about 2½ cups

Rib Mop

1 cup cider vinegar

1 cup water

¼ cup Moppin' Dry Rub (page 20)

1 tablespoon yellow mustard

1 teaspoon Worcestershire sauce

In a medium bowl, whisk together all the ingredients until smooth. Store in an airtight container in the refrigerator for up to 5 days.

This is a version of the recipe I included in my first book, *Smokin' in the Boys' Room*. I have always called it my "BBQ Mother Sauce" as it is very adaptable to adding other flavor components to complement the specific meat I am using or the flavor profile of the geographic area where I am cooking. I have cut down the sweeteners in this recipe, which will make it more adaptable for those who aren't inculcated in the Memphis-style barbecue heritage. Several recipes in the book will use this as a base and add some more flavoring to accentuate the specific recipe.

Memphis-style barbecue utilizes sauce as an integral part of barbecue more closely than some other regions of the country; however, it also highly values how the sauce flavors "marry" with the meat item. This is why the main seasoning component in the sauce is Basic "Memphis-Style" BBQ Rub (page 17) as it will help amplify the flavors you are using in your meat. If you are going to use a different rub, you can try using that instead in the sauce to help complement your entrée. If you want to make a finishing glaze for ribs or other smoked items, mix ½ cup of sauce with 2 tablespoons honey and whisk. This will give your finished product a beautiful sheen as well as an added boost of flavor.

Makes about 6 cups

BBQ Mother Sauce, Version 2

¼ cup peanut or canola oil

¾ cup finely diced sweet or yellow onion

2 tablespoons minced garlic

1½ cups ketchup

¼ cup honey

2 tablespoons tomato paste

⅓ cup white vinegar

¼ cup light brown sugar

¼ cup Worcestershire sauce

2 teaspoons dry mustard

1 teaspoon cayenne

1 teaspoon freshly ground black pepper

½ cup Basic "Memphis-Style" BBQ Rub (page 17), or more to taste

1 cup water, as needed for the desired consistency

In a medium saucepan, heat the oil over medium heat. Add the onion and sauté until translucent, about 4 minutes. Add the garlic and cook for 2 minutes longer. Add the ketchup, honey, tomato paste, vinegar, brown sugar, Worcestershire, dry mustard, cayenne, black pepper, and BBQ Rub and stir well. Simmer for 10 to 15 minutes to thicken and marry the flavors. Slowly add the water, ¼ cup at a time, and stir in until your desired consistency is achieved. A thick consistency is best. Taste and adjust the flavor by adding more BBQ Rub if desired. Cool and store in an airtight container in the refrigerator for up to 10 days.

Tamarind concentrate or paste is sometimes hard to find, but is well worth it. Look at higher-end grocery stores in the Asian foods section, although I am seeing it more and more in local stores. It provides a "needs something" bit of flavor without overwhelming. I have been using it more and more in many of my sauces, but it really helps a steak sauce. This sauce is a mainstay in my refrigerator and gets used for much more than steak.

Makes about 2 cups

Homemade Steak Sauce

1 tablespoon olive oil

¼ cup minced yellow onion

1 bay leaf

1 teaspoon minced garlic

1 cup ketchup

2 tablespoons Worcestershire sauce

Juice of ½ lemon

2 tablespoons white wine vinegar

1 tablespoon packed dark brown sugar

1 tablespoon coarsely ground mustard

1 tablespoon tamarind concentrate or paste

½ teaspoon ancho chile powder or dark chili powder

½ teaspoon kosher salt, or to taste

½ teaspoon freshly ground black pepper

In a small saucepan over medium-high heat, heat the olive oil, add the onion, and sauté until tender, 3 to 4 minutes. Add the bay leaf and garlic and cook until golden, 2 minutes. Add the ketchup, Worcestershire, lemon juice, vinegar, brown sugar, mustard, tamarind, chile powder, salt, and pepper. Bring to a boil, then decrease the heat to simmer for 5 to 10 minutes. Remove the bay leaf. Store in an airtight container in the refrigerator for up to 1 week.

For you non–"Dr. P" fans, you can make this with any soda you like, but the sauce will absolutely not taste like Dr. Pepper if you use it. It just adds a nice "What's in that?" flavor to the sauce, but certainly doesn't overpower it.

Makes 2 cups

Dr. Pepper BBQ Sauce

2 tablespoons unsalted butter

½ cup finely minced white onion

1 tablespoon minced garlic

¼ cup cider vinegar

1½ cups ketchup

¼ cup Worcestershire sauce

2 tablespoons packed light brown sugar

2 tablespoons Basic "Memphis-Style" BBQ Rub (page 17) or your favorite barbecue seasoning

1 teaspoon ancho chile powder or medium-hot chili powder

½ teaspoon granulated garlic

½ (12-ounce) can Dr. Pepper

In a small saucepan, melt the butter, then sauté the onion for 3 minutes over medium-high heat. Add the minced garlic and cook for 2 to 3 minutes, until the garlic is golden. Add the vinegar and cook for 1 minute. Then add the ketchup, Worcestershire, brown sugar, barbecue rub, chile powder, granulated garlic, and Dr. Pepper. Bring to a light boil, then lower to a simmer for 30 minutes to an hour, or until reduced by one-third and the flavors are integrated. Let cool, then use or store in an airtight container in the refrigerator for up to 5 days.

Mississippi Comeback Sauce is a "kissing cousin" to rémoulade sauce. This version has a bit of a kick that goes nicely with crab cakes or any type of seafood. In the words of *The Beverly Hillbillies*, "Y'all come back now, ya hear!"

Makes about 2 cups

Mississippi Comeback Sauce

¼ cup chili sauce

1 tablespoon finely diced red onion

1½ teaspoons minced garlic

¼ cup ketchup

1 tablespoon Worcestershire sauce

1 teaspoon whole-grain mustard

1 cup mayonnaise

1 teaspoon coarsely ground black pepper

1 teaspoon Roasted Pepper Hot Sauce (page 29) or Louisiana brand hot sauce

Juice of ½ lemon

In a small bowl, whisk together all the ingredients. Cover and refrigerate for 30 minutes before serving. Store in an airtight container in the refrigerator for up to 5 days.

I have grown to love different finishing salts, especially flaked salts. Generally these are not used during the cooking process but rather sprinkled on at the end to give some added flavor and texture. Making smoked salt is a fun way to add some flavor and is so simple and easy. I always do this while I'm smoking other items, so no need to fire up the cooker just for this. I have found you can get a nice hint of smoke in the salt in as little as an hour, although much longer is better.

Makes 1 cup

Smoked Sea Salt

1 cup flaked sea salt

Prepare a smoker to cook at 250°F. Different woods will flavor the salt differently, but I prefer cherry or apple wood smoked salt. If you have a dry-heat smoker, put a water pan in the cooker. Place the salt in a pie pan or other ovenproof shallow container and place in the smoker. A disposable aluminum pie pan works well because you can fold it in half to funnel the salt into a storage container. Allow to smoke for 6 to 8 hours, if possible, stirring every hour. Remove the pan from the smoker and allow to cool completely. Pour into an airtight container. Use within 2 weeks for maximum flavor.

MELISSA'S TIP

I always try to think about using smokers as efficiently as possible. There are many things I smoke that really aren't worth firing up a smoker by themselves. Smoking salts, peppers, or other types of specialty products are good items to "hitch a ride" in the smoker, along with other fast-cook items such as tomatoes or fruit. I call these items "hitchhikers" and am always trying to find a spot for them.

For those hardy souls who really love hot sauces, I recommend making an aged, or fermented, hot sauce. Louisiana-style (my favorite) hot sauces are made from a pepper mash that's aged for years before being strained and bottled. These sauces will have a richer, more complex flavor than you can get from a quicker-made sauce. However, this recipe will be ready in a couple of hours, and it gets better sitting in the fridge for the next month. That's a whole lot of time I get to spend enjoying dishes rather than waiting on sauce! Feel free to substitute different types of peppers depending on your heat preference. For this recipe, I wanted the sauce to be red, so I'm using red jalapeños and serranos.

When handling peppers, always wear gloves and wash your hands thoroughly afterward.

Makes about 2 cups

Roasted Pepper Hot Sauce

10 red jalapeño chiles

10 red serrano chiles

1 habanero chile (optional)

2½ cups white vinegar

1 teaspoon kosher salt

4 cloves garlic

½ medium red onion, chopped

On a hot grill, roast all the chiles until blackened, turning as the skin blisters, 8 to 10 minutes. Carefully remove them from the grill and put them into a paper bag or container and cover for 20 minutes. Peel off the skin, then stem and seed all the chiles. Put the chiles in a medium stockpot and add the vinegar, salt, garlic, and onion. Bring to a boil, then decrease the heat to simmer for 20 minutes. Turn off the heat and let sit until cool. Pour the contents of the stockpot into a blender or food processor and purée for 2 to 3 minutes, until very smooth. Pour through a fine-mesh strainer placed over a pot. Press lightly to release as much of the juices as possible. Pour the liquid into a bottle, which should keep in the fridge for up to 1 month.

This has a nice "sneaky heat" from the chipotle and a brightness from the fresh jalapeño. If you want to lower the heat, you can omit either of those chiles and just use a whole red bell pepper. This is my favorite dipping sauce for Southern Meat Pies (page 42) but makes a great dipping sauce or spread for just about any sandwich or appetizer.

Makes 1 cup

Triple-Pepper Aioli

2 large egg yolks

2 tablespoons Dijon mustard

2 teaspoons fresh lemon juice

½ red bell pepper, roasted, peeled, and seeded

½ jalapeño chile, roasted, peeled, and seeded

1 teaspoon diced canned chipotle chile packed in adobo sauce

½ cup extra virgin olive oil

½ cup canola or other neutral-flavored oil

½ teaspoon kosher salt

½ teaspoon coarsely ground black pepper

Put the egg yolks, mustard, lemon juice, bell pepper, and chiles in a food processor and blend for 30 seconds, or until the peppers are finely chopped. You may need to scrape down the sides of the work bowl. In a mixing cup, combine the oils. With the food processor running, slowly drizzle the oils into the mixture, forming an emulsion. Season to taste with salt and pepper. Store in an airtight container in the refrigerator for up to 2 days.

This makes a subtly spicy mayo, not too spicy but just enough to light up the other flavors. The easy way is to just mix some puréed chipotles in with mayo, but that's not really fun, now, is it?

Makes 1 cup

Chipotle Aioli

2 egg yolks

1 tablespoon fresh lime juice

1 teaspoon minced garlic

½ teaspoon salt

2 medium canned chipotle chiles, minced, plus

1 teaspoon adobo sauce

¾ cup olive oil

Place all the ingredients, except the olive oil, in a blender or food processor. Pulse until the chiles are puréed. Scrape the sides if necessary. With the food processor running, slowly drizzle the oil into the mixture, forming an emulsion. Store in an airtight container in the refrigerator for up to 2 days.

CHAPTER 3

APPETIZERS, SMALL BITES, AND SNACKS

Appetizers, snacks, and the like are really my favorite category when dining. I'm the type of person who goes to a restaurant and orders multiple appetizers to share and taste and then skips an entrée. I love the small plates and tapas movement, as that just gives me more opportunities to try things without filling up on any one thing.

An appetizer lets you be creative without having to follow certain rules, such as "I can't serve two starches" or "What vegetable pairs with this meat?" There aren't any rules other than to make it flavorful and fun. Many of the recipes here call for combining different things, such as making Smoked Bell Pepper Relish (page 36) and dressing Butter Bean Pâté (page 34) with it. Generally, I like to keep relishes, pickles, and different sauces that I've made in the fridge and mix and match to provide some flavor contrast to whatever I'm cooking.

Boiled peanuts always bring back childhood memories for me. I can still smell the raw peanuts clinging to the dirt as we pulled them from the ground. My grandfather always saved a couple of rows in his garden for peanuts because he knew I loved them so much.

Drive through many parts of the South and you will definitely find boiled peanut stands, usually with hand-painted signs, outdoor propane burners with huge kettles, and a couple of fellas wearing overalls. Stop and get some fresh, hot boiled peanuts and you will be a fan forever. This recipe requires raw peanuts, which are usually harvested in August. WARNING! These are addictive.

Makes 8 cups

Boiled Peanuts

8 cups raw peanuts in the shell

¼ cup kosher salt

15 cups water

Place the peanuts, salt, and 12 cups of the water in a nonreactive container. Place a plate on top of the peanuts to keep them submerged and soak overnight. Pour the peanuts and water into a large stockpot along with 3 additional cups of water. Bring to a boil, then decrease the heat to medium to maintain a steady boil for 3 hours, adding more water if necessary. Allow to cool (this never happens) and enjoy. Store these in the brine in an airtight container in the refrigerator for up to 1 week, though they are best eaten quickly.

Perhaps I have been misled all of my life, but the beans that I refer to as "butter beans" are evidently known as baby lima beans to the rest of the world. "Butter beans" seems to refer to larger lima beans, which I don't care to use. Since butter bean pâté seems to just roll off the tongue like gravy off mashed potatoes, I'm going to keep calling them that. This recipe makes a unique dip that speaks of summertime and freshness. Canned lima beans can be used, but a true Southerner would never recommend that.

Makes about 3 cups

Butter Bean Pâté

3 cups shelled fresh lima beans

2 teaspoons salt, divided

3 cloves garlic

½ teaspoon freshly ground black pepper

¼ cup chopped fresh parsley

2 teaspoons diced fresh tarragon leaves

¼ cup extra virgin olive oil

Smoked Bell Pepper Relish (page 36), for serving

Assorted crackers, for serving

Place the beans, 1 teaspoon of the salt, and enough water to cover in a medium saucepan and cook over medium heat until tender, about 45 minutes. Remove from the heat, drain the beans, reserving about 2 tablespoons of cooking liquid, and let cool.

Place the beans, the remaining 1 teaspoon of salt, the garlic, black pepper, parsley, and tarragon in a food processor and process until smooth. Add 1 tablespoon of the reserved cooking liquid and process. If the mixture looks too dry, add the other tablespoon of cooking liquid and process. With the processor running, slowly pour in the olive oil until incorporated. Remove from the processor, top with red pepper relish, and serve with assorted crackers.

This is one of those "hitch a ride in the smoker" items I like to make (see page 28). When you have room, take these peppers along for a ride, you'll be happy you did. As I roast and skin the peppers before smoking them, the temperature of the smoker is not really important. The process is more about imbuing the peppers with some smoke flavor. This relish is great served over cream cheese with crackers or on top of Butter Bean Pâté (page 34).

Makes 1½ cups

Smoked Bell Pepper Relish

2 large red bell peppers

1 red serrano chile (optional, for heat)

1 medium red onion, finely diced

1 cup sugar

¾ cup cider vinegar

Using the open flame of a gas burner (or your oven set to broil), roast the peppers to blister the skin all over. Place the peppers in a sealed container for 10 minutes, then remove the skin.

Arrange the peppers in a small aluminum foil pan and place in a 250°F smoker with heavy smoke. Smoke for 30 minutes, then remove.

Seed the peppers, then cut the bell peppers into thin slivers and finely dice the serrano if you're using it. In a small saucepan over medium-high heat, cook the peppers with the onion, sugar, and vinegar for 5 minutes, until the sugar dissolves. Then turn the heat to medium-low and simmer just below a boil for 20 minutes, until the liquid has reduced by one-third and the relish has thickened. Remove from the heat and let cool. Store in an airtight container in the refrigerator for up to 1 week.

While chorizo is the traditional protein to use in *queso fundido*, I love grilling shrimp and using them instead. My Spicy Agave Grilled Shrimp (page 136) works wonderfully with this, and I will save a few shrimp to grill just for this.

Makes 3 cups

Grilled Shrimp Queso Fundido

1 teaspoon butter

2 tablespoons minced red onion

½ teaspoon minced garlic

1 teaspoon flour

⅓ cup milk

½ teaspoon freshly ground black pepper

3 cups cotija or Monterey Jack cheese

6 Spicy Agave Grilled Shrimp (page 136), chopped

Candied Jalapeños (page 47)

Smoked Bell Pepper Relish (page 36)

Fresh cilantro leaves, lightly chopped, for garnish

Tortilla chips, for serving

Place a 6-inch cast-iron skillet over a hot grill and melt the butter in it. Stir in the onions and cook until softened, 3 to 4 minutes. Add the garlic and brown slightly, 3 to 4 minutes. Stir in the flour until incorporated, then pour in the milk, stirring briskly to completely combine with the flour. While stirring, let come to a slight boil and thicken. Move the skillet to a cooler part of the grill and add the cheese, about ⅔ cup at a time, letting each addition melt completely, stirring occasionally, before adding more. After all the cheese is added and melted, transfer to a shallow serving bowl. Top with the chopped shrimp, Candied Jalapeños, and Smoked Bell Pepper Relish and garnish with cilantro. Serve with tortilla chips.

Sometimes I think my life was better when I could enjoy Caesar dressing without knowing that anchovies were what gave it such a wonderful "umami" flavor. Ignorance can be bliss! The anchovies are optional in this recipe, but you won't technically have Caesar dressing if you omit them. I love the look these bowls give to this salad, and I must admit that I can't help eating the bowl first! You can also make bowls in a skillet, but I tend to get better formations by cooking the bowl in a microwave. If you don't want to take the bowl route, you can easily make Parmesan crisps this way to garnish a salad.

Lightly grilling the romaine gives an unexpected contrast in warmth and allows it to pick up some flavor from the grill. I love putting different textures or using temperature in unexpected ways, so this salad fits the bill for me.

Serves 4

Grilled Caesar Salad with Chile Powder Croutons in a Parmesan Bowl

CHILE POWDER CROUTONS

1 teaspoon ancho chile powder

1 teaspoon salt

½ teaspoon freshly ground black pepper

2 tablespoons olive oil

2 cups torn or cut bread (such as Italian or French) in 1-inch pieces

CAESAR DRESSING

1 (2-ounce) can anchovy fillets in oil, drained

4 cloves garlic

2 large egg yolks

2 teaspoons Dijon mustard

¼ cup freshly squeezed lemon juice

1 teaspoon coarsely ground black pepper

½ teaspoon kosher salt, or to taste

½ cup olive oil

PARMESAN BOWLS

2 cups shredded Parmesan cheese, plus extra for serving

½ teaspoon coarsely ground black pepper

GRILLED ROMAINE

4 romaine lettuce hearts, stems intact (or whole heads of romaine, tough outer leaves removed)

½ cup olive oil

continued

To prepare the croutons, preheat the oven to 375°F. In a small bowl, mix the chile powder, salt, pepper, and olive oil. Lay out the bread pieces on a baking sheet and drizzle with the olive oil mixture, then toss to coat all sides. Bake for 10 to 12 minutes, tossing after 5 minutes, to toast until golden brown on all sides. Remove from the oven and let cool.

To make the dressing, in a blender pulse the anchovy fillets, garlic, egg yolks, and mustard. Add the lemon juice, pepper, and salt and pulse to incorporate. With the blender running on low, slowly pour in the olive oil to form an emulsion. Remove and place in a small bowl until ready to serve.

To make the Parmesan bowls, start with 2 large salad bowls that "nest" or fit tightly together to make a nice-sized bowl for the Parmesan. On a 10-inch square of parchment paper, spread ¼ cup of the Parmesan in a circle approximately 7 to 8 inches wide. Lightly sprinkle with some of the black pepper, then microwave on high for 90 seconds. Remove, trying to keep the parchment paper taut. Center the paper over the open bowl, then use a second, slightly smaller bowl to press down the cheese and mold it into the bottom bowl. Flip the bowls, wait 1 minute, then remove the top bowl and the parchment paper, then carefully remove the Parmesan bowl and set aside. Repeat 3 more times with the remaining Parmesan.

To prepare the lettuce, preheat a grill to cook at a medium-hot level. Brush the outer romaine leaves with olive oil, then place on the grill and grill, rotating the lettuce so all sides get marked, just until nice grill marks form, about 1 minute per side.

To serve, arrange the Parmesan bowl on a small salad plate. Take the grilled romaine and cut approximately 1 to 1½ inches from the bottom to remove the core. Hold the leaves together and place inside the bowl standing up. Place a few croutons around each lettuce and drizzle with the dressing. Sprinkle with Parmesan cheese and serve.

This is a great use of any leftover brisket slices you may have, but they have to have enough texture in them to hold together when rolled. If the brisket was all consumed in a mad, beef-induced feeding frenzy, you can easily substitute bacon. A pepper corer will help make short work of the jalapeños.

Makes 12

Brisket Poppers

12 medium-size jalapeño chiles

3 tablespoons Pimiento and Cheese (page 96)

12 slices Beef Brisket Flat (page 98), about 4 inches long

2 tablespoons BBQ Mother Sauce, Version 2 (page 24)

On a hot grill or under a broiler, grill the chiles and blister the skin on all sides. Remove them from the heat and place in a resealable plastic bag and seal. Let sit for 5 to 10 minutes, then remove the skins, stem, and seeds. Carefully stuff the chiles with pimiento and cheese so as not to break them apart. Wrap a piece of brisket around each pepper and secure with a toothpick. Then set into a muffin pan to hold the pepper upright using the toothpicks as "arms." Place the poppers on a cooler part of the grill and cook for 10 to 15 minutes, or until hot all the way through. Remove, lightly brush the brisket edges with BBQ sauce, and serve.

Similar to empanadas, meat pies are most often found in Louisiana. Occasionally a road trip has turned into a wonderful culinary journey for me as I have traveled the "Tamale Trail of Mississippi" and then journeyed into Louisiana and eaten some wonderful meat pies. A spicy meat pie can usually stand on its own, but a nice sauce goes quite well with it. Serve with my Triple-Pepper Aioli (page 30) and you will make these a regular in your rotation. These can also be made in an oven, but cooking on a ceramic smoker like a Big Green Egg using a baking stone will make them extraordinary.

Makes 8 pies

Southern Meat Pies

FILLING

1 teaspoon peanut oil

1 pound ground beef

½ cup diced white onion

1 tablespoon minced garlic

½ cup diced celery

½ cup diced green bell pepper

½ teaspoon cayenne

1 teaspoon hot sauce, preferably Louisiana brand

1 teaspoon freshly ground black pepper

2 teaspoons salt

1 tablespoon flour

1 cup beef stock

DOUGH (YOU CAN USE PREMADE PIE DOUGH, BUT THIS WILL BE BETTER)

2 large eggs, divided

1 tablespoon water

2 cups all-purpose flour

1 teaspoon salt

⅓ teaspoon baking powder

¼ cup solid shortening

⅓ cup milk

Chipotle Aioli (page 30), for serving

To prepare the filling, heat the oil in a large skillet over medium-high heat, then add the beef and cook until browned. Add the onion, garlic, celery, bell pepper, cayenne, hot sauce, black pepper, and salt and cook until the vegetables are soft, about 10 minutes. Add the flour to the beef stock and whisk, then pour into the skillet and cook until the beef mixture is thickened, 2 to 3 minutes. Remove the skillet from the heat and let cool.

To prepare the dough, crack 1 egg into a small bowl, add 1 tablespoon water, and whisk to make an egg wash. Set aside.

Place the flour, salt, and baking powder in a bowl and blend with a fork. Cut in the shortening until it is BB pellet–sized. Lightly whisk the remaining egg, then add the milk and stir. Pour into the flour, a little at a time, stirring each time. Keep stirring until the dough is thick and all the ingredients are incorporated.

To assemble, divide the dough into 8 balls, then place 1 at a time on a lightly floured surface and roll out into roughly a 5-inch circle. Place ¼ to ⅓ cup of the meat mixture into the center of each circle, then brush the outside ⅓ inch with the egg wash and carefully fold the dough over the meat and crimp the edges together with a fork. Repeat with the remaining dough and filling.

Place the pies on a greased baking sheet and chill in the refrigerator for 30 minutes to firm up. Preheat a grill to cook at 400°F, preferably with a baking stone, but if not you can cook over indirect heat on the baking sheet. Remove the pies from the fridge and make 2 to 3 small slits on the top of each pie, then brush the tops with the remaining egg wash. Bake on a stone on the grill for 30 minutes, until golden brown and the dough is fully cooked. Let cool for a few minutes and serve with Chipotle Aioli as a dipping sauce.

Before the first frost, my grandmother would pick any remaining green tomatoes and store them wrapped in newspaper. It was almost like Easter for the kids except we were searching for the last hidden tomatoes instead of eggs.

Smoking a green tomato will help tame some of the bitterness as well as give it a more nuanced effect. This soup is served cold on a hot summer day and is best enjoyed with a tall glass of sweet iced tea and half of a Smoked Chicken Salad (page 110) sandwich.

Makes 2 quarts

Smoked Green Tomato Soup

2 pounds green tomatoes, cored and cut in half

2 tablespoons olive oil, divided

2 teaspoons kosher salt, divided

1 teaspoon coarsely ground pepper

1 large green bell pepper, quartered and seeded

½ cup diced celery

2 bay leaves

½ cup diced Vidalia or sweet onion

2 tablespoons minced shallot

5 cups chicken stock

1 tablespoon honey

¼ teaspoon white pepper

2 cups arugula

1 tablespoon fresh thyme leaves

¼ cup fresh basil leaves

½ cup heavy cream

Prepare a smoker to cook at 250°F. Place the green tomatoes on a sheet pan cut-side down. Score an X on each one, then drizzle 1 tablespoon of the olive oil on the tomatoes and sprinkle with 1 teaspoon of the salt and the black pepper. Add the green bell pepper to the pan and place in the smoker for 1 hour, or until the tomatoes are soft.

Remove the sheet pan from the smoker and set aside. In a stockpot, heat the remaining 1 tablespoon of olive oil and add the celery, bay leaves, and onion. Sauté for 2 to 3 minutes, until the onion is translucent. Add the shallot and cook for 2 minutes, then add the chicken stock, the remaining 1 teaspoon salt, the tomatoes, honey, and white pepper. Bring to a boil and decrease the heat to simmer. Continue to cook until the tomatoes are very soft, about 30 minutes, then turn off the heat. Add the arugula, thyme, basil, and cream and purée with an immersion blender (or pour into a food processor or blender and purée). Let cool and then refrigerate for 6 to 8 hours or overnight to chill. Serve cold with a Smoked Chicken Salad or grilled cheese sandwich.

This makes a great appetizer to set on the table during the big game. The pickled grilled onions and candied jalapeños bring a lot of different flavors to the party. The great thing about nachos is that you can customize them however you wish to fit your palate. I must include a caveat about this recipe. I have a great hatred of canned cheese sauce. I'm not sure where that began, but I can't walk by it at the grocery without giving it a snarl and an ugly look, so while you may substitute your favorite cheese in this recipe, please stay away from the canned cheese sauce.

Makes 1 big honking plate of nachos. How many people you let have some is up to you

Pulled Pork Nachos with Pickled Grilled Onions and Candied Jalapeños

6 to 8 ounces tortilla chips

8 ounces Pulled Pork (page 57), warmed

2 tablespoons BBQ Mother Sauce, Version 2 (page 24)

¼ cup shredded cheddar cheese

1 cup shredded lettuce

2 tablespoons Pickled Grilled Onions (recipe follows)

1 tablespoon Candied Jalapeños (page 47)

On a large platter, arrange the chips in a mound. Top with the pulled pork, a drizzle of BBQ sauce, then sprinkle with the cheddar and lettuce. Top with Pickled Grilled Onions and Candied Jalapeños.

Pickled Grilled Onions

Makes 2 (12-ounce) jars

2 medium red onions

1½ teaspoons olive oil

2½ cups cider vinegar

½ cup plus 2 tablespoons sugar

2 cloves garlic, lightly crushed

1½ teaspoons coarsely ground black pepper

¼ teaspoon cayenne (more if you like heat!)

¾ teaspoon cumin seeds, lightly cracked

2 teaspoons kosher salt

Slice lengthwise through the onions and trim off the stem end, then remove the outer skin and quarter, leaving the root end intact. Lightly brush with olive oil and place cut-side down on a hot grill for 4 minutes, or until you get a nice grill mark. Turn over to get grill marks on the other side, then place the onions on a pan and set aside to cool.

Trim off the root and thinly slice into strips. In a stockpot, bring the vinegar, sugar, garlic, black pepper, cayenne, cumin, and salt to a boil. Decrease the heat to simmer for 10 minutes, ensuring the sugar is fully dissolved. Add the onions and continue to simmer for 10 minutes. Using tongs, remove the onions and place in sterilized jars, filling as full as possible without crushing the onions, then pour the pickling liquid over them. Fasten the lids and store in the fridge for up to 1 month.

Candied Jalapeños

Peppers have their own thermostat to determine heat levels, held mostly in their seeds and membranes. If you want a milder heat, just core the peppers before slicing them, or leave in some seeds and core some if you're a "middle of the road" person. If you are a canner, these can be canned and stored for up to a year. I'm not, so I just enjoy them for a month or so and then make more!

Makes about 2 (8-ounce) jars

1 pound fresh jalapeños

1 cup cider vinegar

2 cups sugar

1 teaspoon granulated garlic

1 teaspoon mustard seeds

2 cloves garlic

1 small white onion, slivered

Wearing gloves, wash, rinse, and stem the jalapeños. Then core them if desired. Cut into 1/8-inch slices. In a small stockpot, bring the vinegar, sugar, granulated garlic, and mustard seeds to a boil. Simmer for 10 minutes to ensure the sugar is fully dissolved. Add the garlic, jalapeños, and onion and simmer for 5 minutes. Using a slotted spoon, transfer the jalapeños and onion to sterilized canning jars, packing as tightly as possible without destroying the slices, then pour the syrup over them. Let cool, then replace the lids and store in the refrigerator for up to 1 month.

I had the pleasure of cooking with chef Bobby Chinn while filming a travel show at the restaurant. The spring rolls we made have a special place in my food memory bank for their subtly smoky yet bold and fresh flavors. I've put my own twist on the dish we created, and it is a showstopper at gatherings due to its unique yet somehow familiar traits.

Makes 8 to 10

Spring Rolls with Chipotle Balsamic Sauce

CHIPOTLE BALSAMIC SAUCE

Makes about 1¾ cups

1 (7.5-ounce) can chipotle chiles in adobe sauce

1 tablespoon fresh lime juice

3 tablespoons honey

2 tablespoons water

⅓ cup plus 1 tablespoon olive oil, divided

½ cup fresh cilantro leaves, lightly chopped

1 teaspoon good-quality balsamic vinegar

SPRING ROLLS

3 cups shredded coleslaw mix (shredded green and purple cabbage, shredded carrots)

½ cup fresh cilantro leaves

1 tablespoon diced scallion

8 to 10 rice papers (spring roll wrappers)

8 ounces lean Pulled Pork (page 57), room temperature or slightly warm

To prepare the sauce, place the chiles, lime juice, honey, water, and 1 tablespoon of the olive oil in a blender. Pulse a couple of times to start breaking up the chipotles and then purée. Add the cilantro and purée. With the blender running on low, drizzle in the remaining ⅓ cup of olive oil until incorporated. Add the vinegar and pulse again. Then pour into a small bowl for dipping.

To make the spring rolls, in a large mixing bowl, toss the coleslaw mix, cilantro leaves, and scallion to combine. Fill a bowl larger than the diameter of the rice paper with cool water. Dip 1 sheet of rice paper in the cool water for about 30 to 45 seconds, until it is just pliable. Place the wrapper on a flat surface, add about ⅓ cup of the coleslaw mix, and roll the edge over and pull back toward you to tighten. Add 1 ounce of the pulled pork, fold both ends over the filled sections, then continue to wrap it tightly. Place the seam side down on a plate and cut in half. Repeat with the remaining wrappers and filling. Serve with Chipotle Balsamic Sauce.

I love the texture of butter lettuce, and about the only thing that makes it better is grilling it! Butter lettuce is also known as Bibb or Boston and is many times sold with the roots intact in a container that allows it to keep living, which greatly increases its freshness. It has a wonderful soft texture but can still withstand some heat on the grill.

Serves 2

Grilled Butter Lettuce and Heirloom Tomato Salad with Southwest Chicken Breast

SMOKED GARLIC VINAIGRETTE

3 whole bulbs garlic

2 tablespoons plus 1 teaspoon extra virgin olive oil, divided

3 tablespoons red wine vinegar

1 tablespoon finely chopped red onion

1 tablespoon honey

1 tablespoon fresh lemon juice

1 teaspoon diced fresh tarragon

1 teaspoon Dijon mustard

¼ teaspoon salt

Freshly ground pepper

SALAD

2 (6-ounce) boneless, skinless chicken breasts

Southwest Spice Blend (page 17) or other seasoning blend

1 head butter lettuce

1 tablespoon olive oil

4 to 5 baby heirloom tomatoes, cored and cut in half

½ medium red onion, cut into wedges

½ cup walnuts

½ cup goat cheese

To make the dressing, first remove the outer skin from the garlic, then thinly slice off the tops and brush with 1 teaspoon of the olive oil. Lay the bulbs on a small pan or sheet of aluminum foil, then place in a smoker or a medium-hot grill (if using indirect method, not directly over heat) at 250°F for 1 hour. Remove when the garlic is softened. Squeeze the softened garlic into a mixing bowl, then add the vinegar, red onion, honey, lemon juice, tarragon, mustard, and salt and whisk. While whisking, slowly drizzle in the remaining 2 tablespoons of olive oil to emulsify, then add pepper to taste.

To make the salad, prepare a medium-hot grill and oil the grates with peanut or other high-smoke-point oil. Season the chicken with a seasoning blend of your choice, place on the grill, and cook for 4 to 5 minutes per side, until the internal temperature reaches 165°F. Remove from the grill and cover lightly with aluminum foil. Set aside to rest.

Cut the lettuce head in half, leaving the stem intact. Brush oil on the cut sides of the lettuce, tomatoes, and onion. Place the cut sides down on the grill. Cook for 2 to 3 minutes, until a light char develops. Remove from the grill and trim off the root end and core of the lettuce.

To serve, place lettuce on each plate, cut-side up, surround with tomatoes, and sprinkle with red onion pieces. Slice the chicken and shingle across the lettuce. Sprinkle the walnuts and goat cheese over each salad. Drizzle some Smoked Garlic Vinaigrette on each salad and serve.

Many grills can handle a pizza, especially if you slightly precook the crust. Pizzas really work well on Big Green Eggs. The ability of a ceramic cooker to hold high temps on a grill gives the pizza a "brick oven" flavor, but usually better! Most brick oven pizzerias use gas to heat their ovens, but on a grill you'll get the authentic wood-fired taste. This dough recipe can handle being rolled thinner to develop a crisp crust. If you like a little more "chew," substitute bread flour to increase the gluten and don't roll it quite as thin.

Sometimes when I'm missing ingredients for a recipe, I substitute unlikely candidates just to see what will happen. The fire-roasted green tomato sauce turned out to be "a winner" and a huge hit with the family, making them happy I didn't have any red tomatoes on hand. *Crema* is a Mexican sour cream that has a thinner consistency than regular sour cream. Sour cream is a fine substitute, thinned slightly with water.

Makes 4 (10-inch) pizzas

Green Tomato Pizza with Smoked Chicken and Truffle Crema

TOOLS

Big Green Egg or other dry-heat grill holding at 600°F

Ceramic pizza stone

Pizza peel

PIZZA DOUGH

1 cup warm water

1 teaspoon sugar

1 teaspoon active dry yeast

3 cups all-purpose flour

1½ teaspoons kosher salt

½ teaspoon dried Italian seasoning (optional)

2 teaspoons olive oil, divided

GREEN TOMATO PIZZA SAUCE

2 tablespoons olive oil

5 medium green tomatoes

½ cup thinly sliced sweet or white onion

2 cloves garlic, minced

1 teaspoon kosher salt

½ teaspoon freshly ground black pepper

1 teaspoon sugar

1 tablespoon white vinegar

2 teaspoons hot red pepper flakes

¼ cup fresh basil leaves, roughly chopped

1 teaspoon diced fresh oregano

TRUFFLE CREMA

½ cup crema

1½ teaspoons white truffle olive oil

TOPPINGS

Enough for 4 small pizzas

8 ounces Smoked Chicken (page 107) or store-bought

½ red bell pepper, slivered

8 ounces fresh mozzarella cheese, cut into thin slices, or 1 cup shredded mozzarella

2 tablespoons fresh corn kernels (drain well if using canned)

4 or 5 fresh basil leaves, lightly chopped

continued

Run warm water until it is around 110°F, then place 1 cup in a small bowl. Add the sugar and whisk, then sprinkle in the yeast and let sit until it blooms, 5 to 10 minutes.

In the bowl of a stand mixer fitted with the dough hook, mix together the flour, salt, and Italian seasoning. Pour in the water/yeast and blend on low speed until combined. Add 1 teaspoon of the olive oil and continue to blend until a dough forms, then keep mixing for 5 or 6 minutes. Lightly flour a cutting board, dump out the dough onto it, and form into a ball. Drizzle the remaining teaspoon of olive oil into a large mixing bowl to coat the inside of the bowl. Transfer the dough ball to the bowl, cover the bowl with a damp towel, and let rise until it doubles in size, about 1½ hours.

While the dough is rising, prepare the sauce. Use 1 teaspoon of the olive oil to lightly oil the green tomatoes and char on a hot grill or on a pan under a broiler, then set aside.

In a small stockpot over medium heat, heat the remaining 1½ tablespoons olive oil, add the onion, and cook until softened, 3 to 4 minutes. Then add the garlic and cook for 2 minutes. Core and chop the tomatoes and add them along with the salt, pepper, sugar, vinegar, and red pepper. Cook for 5 minutes, then decrease the heat and simmer for 25 to 30 minutes, stirring occasionally, until the tomatoes are soft. Stir in the basil and oregano, then, using an immersion blender (or food processor), blend until smooth.

To make the crema, whisk the crema and truffle oil together. Store covered in the refrigerator until ready to use.

When the dough has risen, place the dough on a lightly floured cutting board and knead 4 or 5 times, then cut the dough into 4 parts. Roll out each piece of dough into a 10-inch circle (the thinner the better).

To assemble, spoon about ½ cup sauce onto each crust and spread with the bottom of the spoon. Slice fresh mozzarella cheese into thin slices and lay on the pizza, then sprinkle pulled smoked chicken, red bell pepper slivers, and fresh corn kernels over the pizzas.

To bake, prepare a ceramic grill to 600°F on indirect heat, preferably with a baking stone (or precook the crust for 2 or 3 minutes on a pan or until it is cooked just enough to hold together, then add toppings and slide directly onto the grill grates for a little more grill flavor). Dust a pizza peel with cornmeal, add a pizza, and slide onto the pizza stone and grill for 5 to 6 minutes, or until the crust is browned and any cheese is melted. Remove and drizzle the Truffle Crema over the pizza, using a fork. Then sprinkle on the basil and serve.

MELISSA'S TIP

Baking stones make great grilling accessories, but you want to be sure to heat them up gradually and not "shock" them as this can lead to cracking. Just place the stone on the grill as soon as possible while the cooker is still at a lower temperature and let it heat up with the cooker.

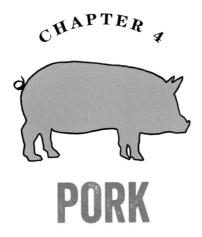

CHAPTER 4

PORK

Growing up, my family had a large smokehouse, and during the winter on the coldest day of the year, they would harvest pigs and process every part of them. The bellies or "middlings," hams, shoulders, and loins would be packed in coarse salt for days and then hung in the smokehouse and smoked over smoldering sawdust. Every part of the pig would be used. Leaf lard, other internal fats, and pieces of belly without "streaks of lean" would be boiled into lard or used with some trimmings to be ground into sausages. This was not about "artisan" meats cured for a restaurant; this was simply trying to survive and not starve through the winter months. Preserving as much of the meat as possible was a necessity.

I still have a deep appreciation for that long, hard process. To this day, the gentle scent of wood smoke brings me back to my childhood and the fond memories of my grandmother Tracy's mother (my great grandmother) and her aunts, uncles, and mother (my great-great grandmother). Maybe these memories laid the foundation for my being drawn into the world of barbecue so strongly, as the fragrant scents of the slowly burning fire connect me with my family. I'm not sure, but I do know I'm at my happiest with a pile of wood, some beautiful pork, and a grill to use. Some of the recipes in this chapter I have been cooking for years; some are fairly recent. They all revolve around my intrinsic appreciation and love for pigs and what they have meant to my family.

One of the oddities today is that we pay more for "natural" pork. Most pork producers raising pigs in a factory setting have little regard for marbling or flavor. Most pork (along with chicken, beef, and almost anything else you can think of) is injected with a brining solution that adds back some flavor to the meat but, more important to the producers, adds weight (remember, you purchase meat by the pound). For producers, this means they can get their stock to market much more quickly than a farmer allowing the animal to put on weight more slowly, which results in better, more marbled cuts. I always try to source humanely raised, natural pork as you will get a much more flavorful piece of meat. Heritage breeds, such as Berkshire, have made a comeback in recent years as people look to the craft farmers to get back to the beautiful textures and flavors of the pork my grandparents and their family raised. Many craft farmers sell their wares at farmers' markets, and supporting them is paramount to increasing the supply. If you get the opportunity to try some Berkshire or other heritage breed pork, I highly recommend that you do.

Pencil sketch by my grandmother, Tracy Pounders

Pulled pork, made by cooking pork butts or shoulders to the perfect temperature and hand pulling the succulent meat, is truly the staple of Southern barbecue. In the world of competition barbecue, we wrap the butts in aluminum foil to preserve color and achieve a certain tenderness level, often at the expense of "bark," the wonderfully flavorful outside crust of the pork. I am a "bark shark," and at home I don't want to sacrifice any of that crust, so in this recipe I cook the butt in a way that I can enjoy the sultry smokiness and flavor of the butt.

Makes 2 to 3 pounds, depending on fat content and size of pork butt

Pulled Pork

1 (8 to 10-pound) bone-in pork butt

¼ cup Basic "Memphis-Style" BBQ Rub (page 17), divided

1 tablespoon yellow mustard

MELISSA'S TIP

If you're concerned about your pork butt getting too dark, want to speed up the cooking process, or would like to add some different flavors to the pork, wrap the butt in heavy-duty aluminum foil after 4 to 5 hours. Reseason according to the recipe, wrap in foil, but before sealing tightly pour ½ cup of apple juice or flavored marinade in with the butt to bring out some different flavors. You will lose some smoke flavor and some of the "barkiness," but that's what the pros do on the contest circuit to keep textures and colors consistent. Don't tell anybody, though, as it's a secret!

Trim any extraneous fat from the side of the butt opposite the fat cap. With the fat cap down, sprinkle 1 tablespoon of the rub on the meat and put 1 tablespoon of the yellow mustard over the seasoning. Rub the seasoning and yellow mustard into the meat, then sprinkle 1 more tablespoon of rub all over the meat. Place in the refrigerator, covered, for 4 to 8 hours, up to overnight. Prepare a smoker to cook at 250°F with pecan, cherry, or apple wood (listed in order of strength of smoke flavor). Place the butt in the smoker fat side down and cook for 5 hours, or until the internal temperature reaches 150°F.

Remove from the smoker, sprinkle the meat with 1 more tablespoon of the rub, and place in a small pan, uncovered. Return to the smoker and smoke for 3 to 4 hours, or until the internal temperature reaches 189° to 192°F and the meat is tender to the touch. Remove from the smoker and let rest in a cooler or Cambro for 1 hour. Wearing "hot gloves," pull the meat apart in small sections and remove any extraneous fat or other unsightly sections. Mix together to incorporate "bark" pieces with the rest of the meat. Lightly sprinkle the meat with the remaining tablespoon of rub, gently toss to combine, and serve.

This flavorful marinade gives an Asian flair to some down-home watermelon and watermelon rind pickles. When we were kids, we'd go out to the watermelon patch and thump watermelons to test for ripeness. When we found the perfect one we would cut a plug (small hole) out of it. When the adults would walk the watermelon patch that day, they'd see the plug and pick the watermelon and we'd "have to eat it." They said they always wondered who was plugging their watermelons, but I can't believe that our guilty faces and giggles didn't give it away. (There was an adult in the bunch with us, but that secret will go with me to the grave.)

Serves 4

Grilled Asian Pork Tenderloin with Watermelon Rind Pickles and Minted Watermelon Salad

Watermelon Rind Pickles
(recipe follows)

TENDERLOIN

⅓ cup soy sauce (lower-sodium soy sauce
may be substituted)

⅓ cup packed light brown sugar

2 tablespoons sesame oil

2 tablespoons fresh ginger, peeled and roughly chopped

1 tablespoon fresh lemon juice

4 cloves garlic, finely chopped

1 tablespoon dry mustard

2 teaspoons coarsely ground black pepper

2 whole pork tenderloins (approximately 1½ to 2 pounds total)

MINTED WATERMELON SALAD

4 cups watermelon, cut into 1-inch cubes (or as close as you can)

1 tablespoon olive oil

1½ teaspoons red wine vinegar

½ medium sweet onion, diced

2 tablespoons chopped fresh mint leaves

Smoked Sea Salt (page 28)

continued

Prepare the watermelon pickles at least a day before you plan to serve them.

To prepare the tenderloins, place all the marinade ingredients in a bowl and whisk until the sugar is dissolved. Place the tenderloins in a large resealable plastic bag and pour the marinade over them. Seal the bag, removing as much air as possible, and refrigerate for at least 6 to 8 hours, up to overnight, turning the bag occasionally.

When almost ready to cook the meat, prepare the watermelon salad. Assemble all the ingredients except the smoked salt in a large mixing bowl and toss gently. Store in the refrigerator until ready to serve.

Set up a grill to cook with direct heat. Remove the tenderloins from the marinade, reserving the marinade. Place the tenderloins on the grill and cook for 12 to 15 minutes, turning every 3 or 4 minutes to cook on all sides, for medium, or until the internal temperature reaches 145°F. Transfer the tenderloins to a plate, cover, and let rest for 5 to 10 minutes.

Strain the remaining marinade over a small saucepan to remove the ginger. Add 2 tablespoons water, bring to a boil, and then decrease the heat to simmer for 2 to 3 minutes.

The sauce should be slightly thickened. (If too thick, add a teaspoon of water at a time until the desired consistency is reached.)

Slice the tenderloin into medallions and drizzle the sauce over them. Sprinkle with watermelon rind pickles and serve with a side of watermelon salad finished with a sprinkle of smoked salt.

MELISSA'S TIP

For those with a chamber vacuum, watermelon is absolutely wonderful "compressed." The texture is changed, and the appearance is like ahi tuna. I love to prepare it this way and put on a salad for a fun visual. You can also infuse other flavors into watermelon by adding juice, balsamic, or other liquid in a chamber vacuum bag with watermelon cubes.

Watermelon Rind Pickles

These will perk up any meal! They take a little effort but are well worth it. This recipe is more of a quick pickle and doesn't involve canning procedures. You will get approximately 2 cups of rind from a very small watermelon. This recipe can be customized very easily as long as the 1:1 ratio of liquid to vinegar is maintained. Try adding basil leaves, ginger, black pepper, or garlic cloves for different flavor combinations.

Makes 1 (12-ounce) jar

½ cup cider vinegar

½ cup water

¼ cup sugar

1½ teaspoons kosher salt

¼ teaspoon cayenne

2 cups watermelon rind, dark green peel removed, cut into very thin slivers

Mix the vinegar, water, sugar, salt, and cayenne in a saucepan and bring to a boil over medium heat. Add the watermelon rind and bring back to a boil. Decrease the heat to simmer for 10 to 15 minutes. Using tongs, place the rinds in a sterilized 12-ounce canning jar, then fill with the pickling liquid until almost full. Seal tightly and refrigerate for 8 hours or overnight for best results before using. Keeps for up to 10 days in the refrigerator.

THE SCIENCE OF SMOKE COOKING

Smoking meats is about cooking low and slow with hardwoods burned down to glowing coals, then shoveling them into a pit. Or it's about cooking hot and fast with lump charcoal and a few wood chunks. And it's about running a wood-pellet-fired cooker at a medium temperature. The reality is the art of barbecue is all of these and more. The "smoke" we see coming from a cooker is really a combination of uncombusted particles from the fuel, gases, and water vapor released from the wood and meat (and water pan, if you are using one). The smoke ring, or the visible effect of cooking meat with wood, is a by-product of a chemical reaction from the gases released by burning wood and proteins in the meat. It has no flavor in and of itself, although it is in an area of the meat that will contain a smoke flavor.

When you are cooking meats, they generally enter a "stall" period, typically around 155° to 160°F, where the internal temperature of the meat stops advancing at a consistent rate. Contrary to general thought, this stall is due to evaporative cooling where liquid from the meat is released on the surface of the meat, evaporates, and thereby cools itself. It is not due to collagens breaking down or fats rendering, although the process of fats rendering can also aid in fluid release in the meat. This is not unique to smoking; however, it is more apparent in barbecue as we are typically cooking larger meats at lower temperatures. An oven baking at 350°F will quickly power through the stall zone, but a smoker at 250°F will obviously take more time. Collagens and other connective tissue are found in greater amounts in muscles that work harder. These muscles, such as pork shoulder, ribs, and beef brisket, form the basis for classic barbecue cuts. Cooking them in a manner such as braising or low-temperature cooking gives the connective tissue enough time to turn from tough to tender. To do this, meats need to be held for a while at an internal temperature of 165° to 205°F, depending on the specific type of meat.

There is truly nothing like an old-school cured and smoked ham. Many of today's hams have been brine injected and fast cured and bear little resemblance to the hams of yore. Barring having a smokehouse, it is a rather arduous task to properly cure and smoke a ham. In this recipe, I skip the curing process and just use a precooked ham but amp up the flavors by putting it through the paces of more smoke and topping it with a delightfully different glaze.

10 to 12 pounds of ham

Smoked Pit Ham with Blackberry-Bourbon Glaze

1 (10 to 12-pound) ham

2 tablespoons Basic "Memphis-Style" BBQ Rub (page 17)

BLACKBERRY-BOURBON HAM GLAZE

Makes about 2½ cups

½ cup bourbon

½ cup apple juice

1 cup seedless blackberry preserves

¾ cup packed light brown sugar

½ cup fresh blackberries (optional, if you don't mind a seed here and there; frozen is fine too)

To prepare the ham, using a knife, score the ham in a crisscross pattern to help the flavors absorb. Rub the ham thoroughly with the seasoning and place in a 250°F smoker under heavy pecan or hickory smoke (I prefer pecan). Smoke for 3 hours.

To prepare the glaze, add the bourbon to a small saucepan. Cook over low heat until reduced by half and the alcohol has evaporated, about 5 minutes. ("Flame the alcohol" at your own risk.) Add the apple juice and preserves and whisk until dissolved. Add the brown sugar and fresh blackberries and continue to stir until the sugar is dissolved and the blackberries have cooked, 4 to 5 minutes. Remove from the heat and use to glaze the ham.

Remove the ham from the smoker and place in a small pan. Brush some of the glaze over the ham and return to the smoker for 20 to 30 minutes, or until the glaze is set. Remove from the smoker, slice, and arrange the slices on a serving platter. You can brush more glaze on the slices or serve it on the side at the table.

Most people love bacon. I tell them they've never had bacon until they've tried it pulled from the side of a 200-pound whole hog cooked low and slow. It truly is amazing when done properly. However, barring an afternoon of just casually cooking a whole hog, I suggest cooking pork belly to get the same sublime texture and flavor. By slowly cooking pork belly and doing a partial braise, you can achieve the texture that makes whole-hog bacon so wonderful.

Serves 4

Smoked Pork Belly with Nectarine–Ginger Ale Glaze and Wilted Spinach

MARINADE

2 cups chicken stock

1½ tablespoons minced garlic

2 cups ginger ale

3 tablespoons honey

1½ tablespoons roughly chopped peeled ginger

1 teaspoon kosher salt if needed

1 teaspoon coarsely ground black pepper

PORK BELLY

2 pounds skinless pork belly, cut into 4 equal squares

¼ cup "Belly Rub" (page 19), plus 2 teaspoons for sprinkling

NECTARINE–GINGER ALE GLAZE

1 cup ginger ale

3 fresh nectarines, peeled, fruit minced

2 tablespoons honey

1 tablespoon grated peeled fresh ginger

½ teaspoon kosher salt

½ teaspoon coarsely ground black pepper

WILTED SPINACH

1½ tablespoons olive oil

1 teaspoon minced garlic

1 pound spinach leaves

Salt and freshly ground black pepper

To prepare the marinade, mix all the ingredients together in a bowl, using the salt only if the stock isn't already salty enough. Place the pork belly pieces in a resealable bag with half of the marinade, reserving the rest for cooking. Marinate for 8 hours, or up to overnight, turning occasionally.

To cook the pork belly, prepare a smoker to cook at 225°F with pecan or fruit wood. Remove the belly pieces from the marinade, pat dry, and rub thoroughly with belly rub, about 1 tablespoon per piece. Place the pieces on the smoker, fat side up, and smoke for 1½ hours.

Remove the belly pieces from the smoker, place in an aluminum foil pan just big enough to hold the meat in one layer without overlapping, pour in the remaining half of the reserved marinade, and cover with foil. Return the pan to the smoker, raise the temperature to 250°F, and smoke for 3 hours.

Meanwhile, prepare the glaze. In a small saucepan over medium heat, reduce the ginger ale by one-third. Add the nectarines, honey, ginger, salt, and pepper and whisk until incorporated. Continue to cook for 3 to 4 minutes, then remove from the heat and set aside.

Check the pork belly by inserting a temperature probe into the meat to check the texture, not necessarily the temperature. It should be tender, like soft butter. Braise longer if necessary. Remove the foil and carefully drain off the marinade, then spoon some of the nectarine glaze over each piece, return the pan to the cooker, and cook for 30 minutes, or until the glaze is reduced and the pork belly is tender. Remove from the pan, lightly spoon more glaze on top of each piece, and rest for 10 minutes.

To prepare the spinach, in a skillet over medium-high heat, heat the oil. Add the garlic and sauté for 1 to 2 minutes. Add the spinach and turn it in the pan so it's coated in oil and begins to wilt. Remove when all the spinach is wilted, about 2 to 3 minutes. Season to taste with salt and pepper.

To plate, using tongs, place a serving of spinach in the middle of each plate. Place a piece of pork belly on top of the spinach, then drizzle the nectarine glaze over and around the pork belly. Lightly sprinkle a pinch of "Belly Rub" over the entire plate.

MELISSA'S
TIP

If you get pork belly with the rind (skin), don't worry as you can follow the same process with a couple of extra steps to make the rind a wonderful textural addition. Before marinating, lightly pierce the rind with a meat maximizer (see page 6) or lightly score the rind in a crisscross pattern, cutting just through the rind. After marinating and seasoning, sear the skin in a hot skillet or on a grill.

This super-simple glaze is flavorful and so easy to make that it has made it onto my "What in the world do I cook for dinner without taking a lot of time?" list. As pork loin easily takes up flavor, it doesn't always require a long marination. The glaze is flavorful enough to carry through to the loin without a marinade, as it's got a nice, spicy bite. The charred okra will happily cook right along with the pork loin, and the dish will go wonderfully with Cool Corn Salad (page 143) or potato salad.

Serves 4

Hot Glazed Pork "Sirloin" with Charred Okra Skewers

1 (2-pound) piece pork loin, from the sirloin end (see Tip, page 67)

1 tablespoon Grillin' Shake (page 22)

2 tablespoons butter

½ cup packed light brown sugar

½ cup medium-spicy hot sauce, such as Louisiana brand

CHARRED OKRA SKEWERS

1 pound fresh medium-size okra

¼ cup olive oil

Juice of ½ lemon

1 teaspoon paprika

1 teaspoon granulated garlic

½ teaspoon salt

½ teaspoon coarsely ground black pepper

½ teaspoon cayenne

To make the pork, cut through the entire length of the pork loin, then cut each half into 2 pieces. Season each piece with Grillin' Shake, then tenderize by using a meat maximizer (see page 6) on both sides, cover, and set aside.

Prepare a medium-hot grill. In a saucepan over medium heat, melt the butter, add the brown sugar, and whisk until dissolved, about 3 minutes. Add the hot sauce, whisk, then lower the heat and simmer for 5 to 10 minutes. Set aside.

Place the pork steaks on the grill and cook for 3 minutes, then rotate a quarter turn. Cook for 2 minutes, then flip. Baste the top side with hot glaze and cook for 3 minutes, then rotate a quarter turn. Remove when the internal temperature is 145°F. Lightly glaze the top again and set aside, covered with aluminum foil to rest.

To make the okra skewers, soak wood skewers, if using, in water for about 30 minutes. Rinse the okra and let it dry. In a small bowl, mix the olive oil, lemon juice, paprika, garlic, salt, black pepper, and cayenne. Place the okra in the bowl and toss to coat. Skewer the okra, about 4 ounces per skewer. (You can use 2 skewers if you don't want them rotating all around, but I generally just use 1.) Place the skewers on a hot grill and cook until tender, about 3 minutes per side. Getting some char on the okra helps the flavor, so don't be afraid! Slide the okra off the skewers and serve.

MELISSA'S TIP

A pork loin has a ribeye end and a sirloin end. The ribeye end is usually the smaller end and will look divided in half with a strip of silver skin and two noticeably different textures of meat. I usually buy a whole pork loin and cut the sirloin end into grilling chops and either cut the ribeye end into frying chops or smoke it whole. Many markets sell half loins, and when possible I always look for the sirloin end to purchase as I think it's a little more versatile, although more prone to drying out. Simply be careful when you cook and serve at a "medium" temperature, 145° to 150°F.

A pork steak, or pork butt steak, is basically a Boston butt cut all the way through like a steak, ¾ to 1 inch thick. I like to give these a double layer of spice and a mini-smoke, then a sear. This takes a bit longer than grilling a steak, but it makes for a flavorful, inexpensive dinner.

Serves 4

Grilled Pork Butt Steak

APPLE MARINADE

2 cups apple juice

2 tablespoons peanut oil

1 teaspoon salt

1 teaspoon coarsely ground black pepper

¼ cup diced white onion

1 teaspoon granulated garlic

GRILLED PORK BUTT

4 (1-inch-thick) pork butt steaks

3 tablespoons Basic "Memphis-Style" BBQ Rub (page 17)

Southwest Spice Blend (page 17)

½ cup BBQ Mother Sauce, Version 2 (page 24), plus more for serving on the side

Combine all the marinade ingredients in a bowl and stir to dissolve the salt. Place the pork butt steaks in a resealable bag and pour the marinade over them. Seal tightly and place in the refrigerator for 8 hours or up to overnight, turning occasionally.

Set up a grill for indirect heat to cook at 275° to 300°F with oak wood. Remove the steaks from the marinade, shake dry, and sprinkle the rub thoroughly on both sides, patting any extra seasoning onto each steak. Place the steaks on the opposite side of the grill from the heat and cook for 1 hour. If using a charcoal grill, maintain a grill with coals and wood through the cooking process to maintain an even heat and preserve fire for the final sear. Flip the steaks to the hot side of the grill and cook for 3 minutes to get a grill mark, then flip and glaze with the sauce. Allow the glaze to set, 3 to 5 minutes, then remove and rest for 5 minutes before serving.

This brings some great flavors and textures together. I grew to love pears only as an adult and now use them as often as I can. I love the combination of pork and pears. Pears are subtly sweet, and the texture is very complementary to the pork loin. Be careful of your cooking temperature with this cut as pork loin can easily dry out; it's best served medium.

Serves 4 to 6

Smoked Pork Loin with Pear and Onion Sauce

1 (3-pound) piece boneless pork loin

3 tablespoons Basic "Memphis-Style" BBQ Rub (page 17), divided

Olive oil

1 cup thinly sliced yellow onion

1½ cups peeled Bosc pears cut into matchsticks

1 tablespoon red wine vinegar

1 teaspoon minced garlic

1 tablespoon butter

1 teaspoon flour

1 cup chicken stock

½ teaspoon salt, or to taste

¼ teaspoon freshly ground black pepper, or to taste

Season the pork loin thoroughly with 2 tablespoons of the rub and then pierce all sides with a meat maximizer (see page 6) to help push the seasoning into the meat and tenderize. Allow to marinate in the fridge, covered, for 4 hours.

Prepare a smoker or a grill for indirect heat to cook at 250°F, with a water pan and hickory wood. Place the loin on the grill and smoke for 45 minutes to an hour, or until the internal temperature is approximately 140°F. Remove from the smoker and set aside to rest for 5 to 10 minutes.

Place a skillet on a burner over medium heat and add a small drizzle of olive oil. Add the onions, pears, red wine vinegar, garlic, remaining 1 tablespoon rub, and butter to the skillet and stir until the onions and pears are softened, about 4 minutes. Whisk the flour into the chicken stock in a small bowl, then pour the mixture into the skillet and cook until reduced by half. Remove from the heat and add salt and pepper. Slice the pork loin into thin slices, shingle 2 or 3 on a plate, spoon the pear-onion sauce over the top of each, and serve.

I have always loved cured items and appreciate the care and skill that some meat artisans put into their craft. Since we opened Memphis Barbecue Company restaurants, we have been curing our own bacon as an homage to some of the people doing things the old-school way. As a happy side effect, I always have a source for wonderful pork bellies, which tend to make life a bit more delicious! By filleting out the pork tenderloin in this recipe, we can cook the porchetta to a higher temperature than we would normally cook pork tenderloin and retain moisture from the basting effect of the belly.

Pork belly with the rind (skin) is traditional and uses a large piece of the belly along with the loin. If you have skin-on belly, simply modify this recipe by piercing the skin with a meat maximizer (see page 6) or lightly scoring it in a crisscross pattern before wrapping it up into a roll. At the end of the cooking process, place it under a broiler or on a hot grill to crisp the skin for a few minutes and give it a wonderful textural contrast.

This is also wonderful on a sandwich topped with fresh arugula and my Chipotle Aioli (page 30).

Makes 8 to 10 beautiful slices

Smoked Pork Belly "Porchetta"

¼ cup fresh basil, chopped

¼ cup fresh oregano, finely chopped

2 tablespoons fresh flat-leaf parsley, finely chopped

1 (2-pound) whole pork loin tenderloin

1 (10 by 12-inch) piece skinless pork belly

1 tablespoon minced garlic

4½ tablespoons "Belly Rub" (page 19), divided

6 thin slices prosciutto

Olive oil

Mix the herbs together on a plate and leave out to dry slightly.

Trim any silver skin off the pork tenderloin and begin to cut it into a flat piece that can be rolled jelly-roll style by slicing lengthwise down the loin about ½ inch deep and then continuing around the meat until the tenderloin is flat. Lay a sheet of plastic wrap over the tenderloin and flatten it with a blunt meat mallet (or your favorite cast iron skillet!) until it is just slightly smaller than your piece of pork belly; set aside.

Lay the pork belly, skin-side down, on a cutting board. Lightly pound the larger areas until it is fairly even. Using a sharp knife, lightly score the belly in a checkerboard pattern. Rub the inside of the belly with the garlic. Season the inside with about 1½ tablespoons of "Belly Rub," then lightly sprinkle with about a quarter of the mixed herbs. Lay the pork tenderloin on top of the belly and season with 1 tablespoon of the rub and again sprinkle with another quarter of the herbs. Lay the slices of prosciutto across the loin, then begin rolling up the assembled porchetta as tightly as possible. After rolling, secure with butcher's twine, brush with olive oil, and thoroughly coat the outside of

continued

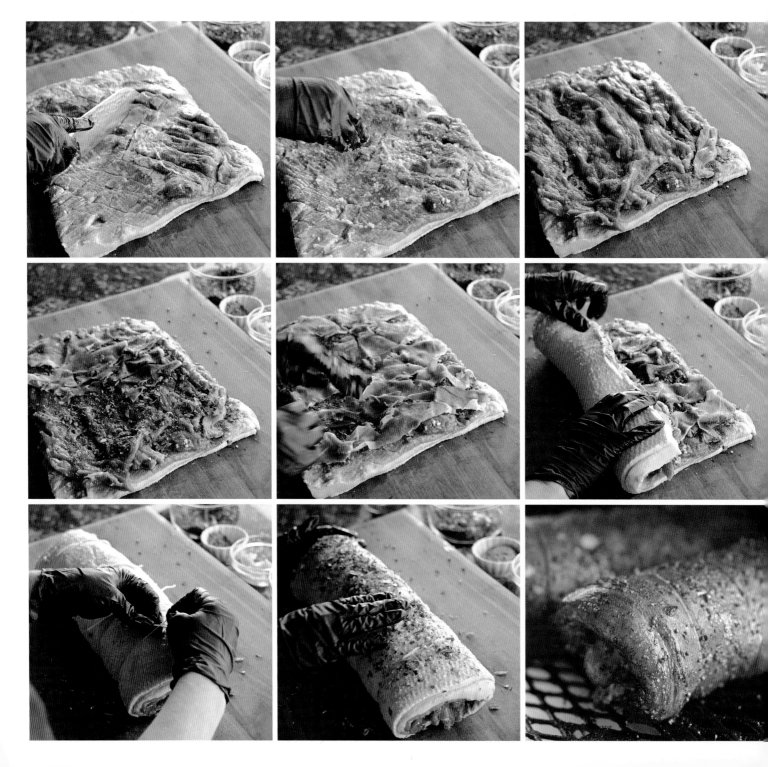

the roll with the remaining 2 tablespoons of belly rub and the remaining half of the herbs. Put in an aluminum pan, cover lightly, and refrigerate for at least 2 hours.

Prepare a smoker to cook at 275°F with cherry and apple wood or other fruitwoods. Remove the porchetta from the refrigerator about 30 minutes before cooking, then place in the smoker. Cook for 2½ to 3 hours, checking occasionally for color and temperature. If the roll is getting too dark, you can lay aluminum foil over the roll for the remaining cooking time. Continue to cook until the internal temperature reaches 170°F. Remove from the smoker, place in a pan, cover lightly with aluminum foil, and let rest for 10 minutes. Slice ¾ to 1 inch thick and serve.

Memphis has a reputation for serving dry ribs. I'm not really sure how that all started, but I can assure you that in the last thirty or so years I have eaten barbecue all over the city, and traditionally those ribs are served wet. However, I can appreciate barbecue without sauce, so sometimes I like to cook ribs with the intent of enjoying the rib meat without the fuss of a sauce.

Most of my competition life I have used water smokers. Because of this, I generally do not baste or "mop" my ribs during the cooking process, preferring to add flavors via rubs or with a flavored liquid while they are wrapped in foil. However, you can add another layer of flavor to your ribs by basting as it allows the mop to reduce on the ribs and concentrate the flavor.

Serves 2 to 4, depending on whether you're feeding cheerleaders or linebackers

Mopped Baby Back Ribs

2 (2 to 2½-pound) slabs baby back ribs

4 tablespoons Basic "Memphis-Style" BBQ Rub (page 17), divided

2 tablespoons yellow mustard

RIB MOP

Makes about 2½ cups

1 cup cider vinegar

1 cup water

¼ cup Moppin' Dry Rub (page 20)

1 tablespoon yellow mustard

1 teaspoon Worcestershire sauce

Barbecue sauce, for glazing (optional)

Remove the membrane from the back of the ribs. Season the back side of each slab with about 1½ teaspoons of the rub, then drizzle on 1½ teaspoons of the mustard and work the seasoning into the meat. Flip the slabs over and repeat, with 1 tablespoon of rub on the meat side of each slab. Place the ribs in a resealable bag or a small pan and place in the refrigerator, covered, 8 hours to overnight.

To make the mop, whisk together all the ingredients in a bowl and store in the refrigerator until ready for use.

Preheat a smoker to cook at 250°F with fruitwood such as apple. Remove the ribs from the refrigerator and let sit out for 30 minutes to come to room temperature. Lightly sprinkle the top side again with about ¾ teaspoon of rub for each slab, then place in the smoker. Cook for 4½ to 5 hours, mopping the tops every 30 to 45 minutes. Remove the ribs when the meat feels tender and pulls away from the bone around ½ inch. If you want to serve a "dry rib," then sprinkle the tops of the ribs with the remaining 1½ teaspoons of rub on each and serve. If you prefer a "wet rib," lightly glaze with BBQ Mother Sauce, Version 2 (page 24) or your favorite barbecue sauce and return to the cooker for 10 minutes for the glaze to tighten up.

For a super-thick piece of meat like a double-cut bone-in pork chop, most restaurants will mark the meat on the grill and then finish in an oven. As most restaurant grills run around 500°F or hotter, it's hard to get it cooked properly without burning the outside. This is easily remedied by running a two-zone cooking fire. You will also generate more flavor, as the smoke from the grill will continue to flavor the chop as it finishes cooking.

Serves 4

Double-Cut Pork Chops with Fresh Peach Chutney and Warm Grilled Potato Salad

4 (10 to 12-ounce) double-cut bone-in pork chops

1 tablespoon peanut oil

¼ cup Grillin' Shake (page 22)

Fresh Peach Chutney (recipe follows)

Grilled Potato Salad, Two Ways (page 77)

Set up a grill for two-zone cooking, with one hot side and one side as indirect heat. Remove the pork chops from the refrigerator 30 to 40 minutes before cooking. Lightly oil the chops, then sprinkle both sides with Grillin' Shake, about 1 tablespoon per chop, and allow them to come up to temperature. Oil the grates, then place the pork chops down on the hot side of the grill and cook for 6 to 7 minutes. Rotate a quarter turn and continue to cook for 6 to 7 minutes. Flip the pork chops and cook for 3 minutes, then move to the cooler part of the grill. It should take another 12 to 15 minutes for the internal temperature of the pork chop to come up to 140° to 145°F. Remove from the grill and cover lightly with aluminum foil to rest for 5 to 10 minutes. Serve on a plate topped with fresh peach chutney, with potato salad on the side.

continued

Fresh Peach Chutney

Makes 2 cups

1 tablespoon olive oil

1 tablespoon minced red onion

2 tablespoons diced red bell pepper

1 teaspoon minced jalapeño or serrano chile (optional)

1 tablespoon minced garlic

½ cup packed light brown sugar

¼ cup cider vinegar

½ teaspoon salt, or to taste

½ teaspoon freshly ground black pepper, or to taste

4 fresh peaches, preferably freestone, peeled and cut into thin wedges

1 tablespoon grated peeled fresh ginger

Heat the oil in a small skillet over medium-high heat, then add the onion, bell pepper, and chile, if using, and cook for 3 to 4 minutes, until soft. Add the garlic and cook until golden, about 2 minutes. Add the brown sugar, vinegar, salt, and pepper and bring to a quick boil. Then lower the heat to simmer until the brown sugar is fully dissolved. Add the peaches and ginger and simmer for 10 minutes, or until the juice has thickened. Remove from the heat and serve. (This keeps for 3 days refrigerated. If made ahead of time, warm before serving with the pork chops.)

Grilled Potato Salad, Two Ways

Make the dressing of your choice ahead of time to add to the potatoes as they get done and are ready to serve. In the heat of summer I usually go with the vinaigrette, but the rest of the year I'm a creamy potato salad girl.

Serves 4

CREAMY DRESSING

1 cup mayonnaise

½ bunch scallions (greens and white parts), chopped

1 teaspoon Dijon mustard

¼ cup minced dill pickle

¼ cup sweet pickle relish

1 tablespoon chopped fresh tarragon

Salt and freshly ground black pepper

VINAIGRETTE DRESSING

½ cup extra virgin olive oil

3 tablespoons white wine vinegar (I like to use a citrus champagne vinegar)

2 tablespoons chopped fresh flat-leaf parsley

2 teaspoons Dijon mustard

1 teaspoon minced garlic

1 tablespoon chopped fresh tarragon

1 bunch scallions (greens and white parts), chopped

Salt and freshly ground black pepper

SALAD

2 pounds new potatoes, halved

2 tablespoons extra virgin olive oil

1 teaspoon kosher salt

½ teaspoon freshly ground black pepper

½ teaspoon granulated garlic

6 slices thick-cut bacon

Prepare one of the dressings, whisking all the ingredients, including salt and pepper to taste, together. Set aside until ready to use.

Mix the potatoes, oil, salt, pepper, and garlic in a large mixing bowl and toss to coat the potatoes with oil. Place the potatoes on a hot grill cut side down. Cook for 2 or 3 minutes, then turn over and continue to cook for 3 minutes. Move the potatoes to an aluminum foil pan on a cooler spot on the grill, cover, and cook for another 10 to 15 minutes, until they are fork tender.

Place the bacon on an area of the grill not directly above the coals but still hot and cook until crispy, 3 to 4 minutes per side. Remove and set aside.

Remove the potatoes from the grill, crumble the cooled bacon, and add to the potatoes in the pan. Add just enough dressing of your choice to coat the potatoes and serve. (As they cool, the potatoes will absorb some of the dressing, so you can add any reserved dressing to leftovers before refrigerating.)

This is easily prepared and makes a beautiful presentation to set on the dinner table before slicing. The stuffing is a favorite of mine as the creaminess of the goat cheese complements the pork quite well. However, any number of different things such as a fresh seasonal fruit or different cheeses will be great in this recipe.

Serves 4 to 6

Pork Loin Purse with Spinach, Pear, and Goat Cheese

1 (3 to 4-pound) piece pork loin

1 tablespoon Basic "Memphis-Style" BBQ Rub (page 17)

¼ medium white onion, thinly sliced

1½ teaspoons minced fresh tarragon

3 cloves garlic, minced

1 Bosc pear, peeled and chopped

½ cup shiitake mushroom caps, thinly sliced

1 teaspoon kosher salt

½ teaspoon freshly ground black pepper

½ cup fresh spinach

½ cup crumbled goat cheese

Preheat a smoker or grill for indirect heat to cook at 275°F. Rinse the pork loin and pat dry. Beginning about ¾ inch from one end and continuing to ¾ inch from other end, cut a slit in the pork loin, about three-quarters of the way into the loin. At the bottom of the cut, make small slices to make a "T" or a pocket. Season the outside of the pork loin with the rub as well as inside.

In a small bowl, combine the onion, tarragon, garlic, pear, mushrooms, salt, and pepper and toss to mix. Stuff the spinach into the pork loin, then pack with the onion-tarragon mixture. Place in the smoker for 1 hour and 15 minutes, until the meat temperature nears 140°F. Sprinkle the goat cheese over the stuffing and cook for another 10 to 15 minutes, until the internal temperature reaches 145°F. Remove from smoker and let rest for 5 minutes before slicing 1 inch thick.

Smoked Short Ribs (page 86)

CHAPTER 5

BEEF

In spite of my deep appreciation for pork, if I had to pick one type of meat to cook for dinner it would be beef. Richly flavored, able to carry heavy spice as well as delicate nuance, beef is significantly more varied than people give it credit for being. Although you will never have to twist my arm for a juicy steak, I enjoy the "lesser" cuts as much as or more than the more popular steaks. While you will never find a filet in my house, if you don't come across some skirt steak, flank steak, or a brisket, it only means I've been out of town for an extended period of time.

The many facets of the different cuts really allow you to change not only what you cook but also how you cook. I love smoking and braising to achieve a tender texture on a short rib, but there's nothing quite like a rotisserie-roasted piece of flank or a marinated and quick-grilled skirt steak. You name the piece of cooking equipment, and I will name you a recipe that will produce sublime beef, and it's not very hard because there are so many. The recipes in this chapter run the gamut of beef cuts, from the underappreciated hanger steak to the barbecue mainstay, beef brisket. I am also including dry-aging beef and smoking a prime rib, something everyone should try. It is definitely one of those culinary processes that seems much harder than it is and really requires only some patience. When it comes to beef, though, patience is sometimes hard to come by!

Flank steak is one of my favorite meats to cook, but throw it on a spit and flame-roast it and I really love it! While I love this on a rotisserie, it is easily adaptable to simple grilling as well.

Serves 4 to 6

Rotisserie Southwest-Spiced Flank Steak with Chimichurri and Grilled Lime-Cilantro Slaw

1 (2-pound) piece flank steak, 1 inch thick if possible

2 tablespoons Southwest Spice Blend (page 17)

Chimichurri Sauce (recipe follows)

Grilled Lime-Cilantro Slaw (page 85)

Tenderize the flank steak on both sides using a meat maximizer (see page 6). Season each side with the spice blend, applying the spice thickly and then patting the spices into the meat. Cover with a paper towel and set aside for 15 to 20 minutes while you heat the grill.

Preheat a grill to cook at 500°F, using a back burner for rotisseries if possible. Thread the flank steak over the spit by rounding the flank steak and piercing it twice with the spit, secure with spit holders, and turn on the rotisserie.

Place on the grill and roast for 15 to 18 minutes (depending on thickness) for medium-rare and 20 to 23 minutes for medium. I have seen a lot of inconsistency in the size and thickness of flank steak, so adjust the times depending on the size you get.

Test the meat with an instant-read thermometer in the thickest part (see doneness chart, page 172). Remove from the spit, cover loosely with aluminum foil, and let rest for 5 to 10 minutes. Thinly slice against the grain approximately ¼ inch thick. Plate 2 to 3 slices (depending on length) per person and spoon some chimichurri sauce over the middle. Serve with more chimichurri on the side and Grilled Lime-Cilantro Slaw.

continued

Chimichurri Sauce

This is a simple garlic and herb relish that goes well with just about any grilled meat, and I think it's rather snappy! This holds for a day or so in the fridge, so it can be made ahead of time, but bring it to room temperature for serving.

Makes about 3 cups

¼ cup minced sweet onion

4 cloves garlic

1 cup fresh flat-leaf parsley

1 cup fresh cilantro leaves

1 tablespoon fresh oregano leaves

½ cup red wine vinegar

½ teaspoon kosher salt, or to taste

¼ teaspoon coarsely ground black pepper

½ cup extra virgin olive oil

1 tablespoon diced fresh jalapeño chile

½ red bell pepper, roasted, seeded, and finely chopped

In a food processor, pulse the onion, garlic, parsley, cilantro, and oregano to purée. Scrape down the sides of the work bowl and add the vinegar, salt, and pepper. Pulse again. With the processer running, slowly pour in the olive oil. Remove from the processor and stir in the jalapeño and red bell pepper, then taste to adjust the salt and pepper.

Let sit for at least an hour to let the flavors meld and then whisk again before serving.

Grilled Lime-Cilantro Slaw

Serves 4 to 6

LIME-CILANTRO VINAIGRETTE

¼ cup fresh lime juice

1 tablespoon cider vinegar

1 tablespoon honey

1 tablespoon minced garlic

½ teaspoon kosher salt

¼ teaspoon freshly ground black
    pepper

1 tablespoon chopped fresh
    cilantro

⅓ cup olive oil

SLAW

1 small to medium head green
    cabbage

¼ cup olive oil

½ cup shredded carrot

1 cup fresh cilantro leaves

Salt and freshly ground black
    pepper to taste

To make the vinaigrette, whisk all the ingredients except the olive oil in a mixing bowl. While whisking, slowly drizzle in the olive oil to form an emulsion. Set aside.

Remove the tough outer leaves of the cabbage head, then quarter, leaving the core. Brush each cut side of the cabbage with olive oil, then place on a hot grill. Grill for 3 to 4 minutes per cut side, or until you get a nice grill mark. Remove from the grill and let cool. Cut out the core and slice down the cut side into very thin strips. Place in a large bowl with the carrot and cilantro. Whisk the dressing one more time and then pour over the slaw and toss to coat evenly.

Although short ribs are one of my favorites, the yield (the edible portion of a product versus the total original weight) is very low, as they contain bones and lots of fat. However, when smoked or braised, the fat will render and baste the meat to create rich pieces of beefy goodness. When smoking short ribs, I usually season them with my Basic "Memphis-Style" BBQ Rub, which works well with the smokiness they pick up. Generally, I get "English-style short ribs" but ask the butcher not to cut them into small pieces so I get large, caveman-worthy ribs.

Serves 4 to 6

Smoked Short Ribs with Grilled Fingerling Potatoes

4 to 5 pounds short beef ribs

Olive oil

2 tablespoons Basic "Memphis-Style" BBQ Rub (page 17)

2 cups beef stock

⅓ cup BBQ Mother Sauce, Version 2 (page 24)

Grilled Fingerling Potatoes (recipe follows)

Prepare a smoker to cook at 250°F. (A grill can be set up to run on indirect heat for this as well, with an aluminum foil boat with wood chips.) For short ribs I prefer to blend hickory and cherry wood equally as they will benefit from a strong smoke flavor.

Brush the ribs with olive oil and season them moderately with the rub. Place in the smoker, bone-side down, and allow to smoke for 2 hours. In a 10 by 12-inch disposable aluminum foil pan, place the ribs bone-side down and add the beef stock to the pan. Cover with aluminum foil and place on the smoker. Cook for 2½ hours, until the meat is fork-tender.

Allow the cooker temperature to drop as the meat is getting more tender, then pour off most of the liquids into a fat separator cup and place in the freezer for 10 minutes to quickly separate the fats. Pour about ⅔ cup of the beef stock and drippings into a small saucepan and boil until reduced to ⅓ cup. Then mix with the sauce and glaze the short ribs. Leave the short ribs in the pan, uncovered, for 10 minutes, then remove from the cooker and allow to rest for 10 minutes before serving with the potatoes.

Grilled Fingerling Potatoes

You can easily do this all in a grilling basket or in an aluminum foil pan, but I like to put grill marks on the potatoes to get some flavor directly on the potatoes and then move them over to a cooler spot in a pan or on foil to finish cooking. I like fingerlings seasoned simply with salt and pepper, tarragon, and garlic, but your favorite herbs or seasoning blend will work.

Serves 4 to 6

2 pounds fingerling potatoes, cut in half lengthwise

1 teaspoon kosher salt, plus more to taste

½ teaspoon coarsely ground black pepper, plus more to taste

2 tablespoons olive oil

1 tablespoon minced fresh tarragon

1 teaspoon minced garlic

Place the potatoes, salt, pepper, and olive oil in a small aluminum foil pan and toss to coat. On a 2-zone grill, lay the potatoes cut-side down for about 3 minutes on the hot zone to develop grill marks, then flip and allow to cook for 3 more minutes. Move the potatoes back to the pan and toss with the tarragon and garlic. Then place on a medium-low area of the grill to finish cooking, about 20 minutes, until fork-tender. Adjust the salt and pepper to taste, if desired.

MELISSA'S TIP

I prefer my short ribs to have a more fork-tender texture, which is why I put them in a pan with some liquid to braise. You can easily just leave them on the smoker to finish, which will yield a smokier flavor and a firmer texture with more of a "bark" effect on the outside.

This dish is absolutely brimming with different flavors and textures. If you can't find hanger steak, you can substitute flank steak as they are similar, but generally hanger steak is more tender. Sweet potatoes are one of my favorite foods, but sometimes they need a contrast, so I season the hanger steak heavily and then grill at high temps to give it a blackened effect. The spiciness of the steak works well against the sweetness of the hash, and the egg ties it all together. Hanger steak, like flank or skirt steak, benefits from a medium-rare to medium temperature.

Serves 4

"Blackened" Hanger Steak with Sweet Potato Hash and Fried Egg

2 (8-ounce) trimmed hanger steaks

3 to 4 tablespoons Blackening Seasoning (page 18)

Sweet Potato Hash and Fried Egg (recipe follows)

Salt and freshly ground pepper

Fresh cilantro sprigs, for garnish

If your steak is not pretrimmed, remove any silver skin and excess fat from each steak. Then cut in half along the middle sinew and trim each steak. Season the steaks heavily and place in the refrigerator, uncovered, for 4 to 6 hours.

Before grilling, remove from the fridge and leave out for at least 30 minutes to dry and come to room temperature. Prepare a grill to cook on high or very hot if using a charcoal grill. For this recipe, my preference is definitely using lump charcoal, as it will burn hotter and still impart a smoke flavor. Oil the grill grates and place the steaks on the grill. Cook for 2 to 3 minutes, then roll one quarter of the way over and repeat for all four sides. Remove from the grill when an instant-read thermometer reads 130° to 135°F in the thickest part of the steak, depending on your temperature preference. Cover lightly with aluminum foil and let rest for 5 to 10 minutes. The temperature of the steak will increase 3° to 5°F while resting.

To plate, place a 5-inch burger ring in the middle of a plate. Fill with the hash, then lightly press to form in the ring (without breaking up the potatoes if possible). Remove the ring, then top the hash with the fried egg seasoned to taste with salt and pepper. Slice the hangar steak against the grain into ½ to ¾-inch-wide strips and shingle pieces around the hash. Garnish with the cilantro sprigs and serve.

continued

Sweet Potato Hash and Fried Egg

This dish can stand on its own and makes a great Sunday brunch item. If you like a little more Southwest feel, use a poblano chile in place of some or all of the bell pepper.

Serves 4

6 slices bacon, cut into pieces

2 medium sweet potatoes, peeled and cut into ½-inch cubes, parboiled and thoroughly drained

2 tablespoons butter

1 cup roughly chopped yellow onion

1 green bell pepper, seeded and cut into slivers

1 teaspoon minced garlic

½ teaspoon salt

¼ teaspoon freshly ground black pepper

6 ounces fresh spinach

1 teaspoon minced fresh thyme

4 large eggs, cooked sunny side up

Cook the bacon in a large, nonstick skillet until crispy, then use tongs to remove the bacon, leaving the rendered fat in the pan.

Turn the heat to medium and cook the potatoes for 5 to 6 minutes, then raise the heat to medium-high and cook for about 5 minutes, or until the potatoes are browned. Keeping the stove on medium-high heat, add the butter to the skillet and cook the onion and bell pepper until softened and browned, 5 or 6 minutes. Add the garlic, cooked bacon, salt, pepper, and spinach and cook until the spinach is wilted, about 3 minutes. Add the thyme and stir carefully to incorporate. Remove the pan from the heat and adjust the seasoning if necessary. Right before plating, fry eggs sunny-side up and serve warm, shingled over sweet potato hash.

Dry-aging beef gives it a richer, fuller flavor, although you do lose some yield to the process. I generally buy a whole ribeye, dry-age it, cut about half into steaks, and smoke the rest as a prime rib, but you can use it all for prime if you're feeding a group. For this recipe you will need to dedicate some refrigerator space for 7 days to a month, depending on your love of the dry-aged flavor (I suggest a minimum of 21 days). A word of caution: Your refrigerator will have a smell to it, so this is best done in a secondary fridge if possible. I generally don't purchase bone-in ribeyes, but they will work well and provide a nice presentation if you choose them.

If you don't want to go through the dry-age process, simply ignore the cheesecloth in the recipe and skip down to the cooking section of the recipe. I also use stronger wood when cooking fresh primes, such as cherry and/or pecan. An internal meat thermometer is key to this recipe as it allows you to check the temperature without opening the smoker many times.

Serves 4 to 8

Dry-Aged Prime Rib with au Jus and Fresh Horseradish Sauce

1 (12 to 14-pound) boneless beef ribeye (well marbled, choice grade or better)

Cheesecloth, for dry-aging

Fresh Horseradish Sauce (recipe follows)

3 tablespoons Fresh Herb Rub (page 20)

Quick Jus (page 93)

To dry-age the beef, do not trim any fat from the ribeye. Pat the ribeye dry, then wrap in cheesecloth, place on a pan toward the back of the refrigerator, and leave, uncovered, for 2 days.

Remove the ribeye, change out the cheesecloth, and return for a minimum of 5 days, up to 26 days. The longer you age it, the more you will have to trim away but the deeper the flavor.

Remove the ribeye and discard the cheesecloth. Trim away any discolored areas and the exposed fat. At this point you may cut into steaks for grilling, smoke as a prime rib, or a combination.

Prepare the horseradish sauce at least 2 to 3 hours before serving.

continued

When ready to cook, preheat a smoker to cook at 250°F with moderate smoke from the wood. Liberally apply the herb rub to all surfaces of the meat, especially packing it on the top. Place in the smoker and cook for 20 to 22 minutes per pound (remember, it doesn't weigh what it did when you started as it has probably lost 20% to 25% of its raw weight), depending on desired doneness. A prime rib that started at 12 pounds, for example, will probably end up being around 9 pounds to smoke, so it will take about 3 hours. After 2 hours, set the prime rib in an aluminum foil pan, but do not wrap (to reserve some drippings) and continue to cook to your desired temperature. Remember, you want to pull the prime rib off 3° to 5°F below your desired temperature (see below), as the internal temp will rise about that much during a resting period. Remove the prime rib from the smoker and let rest for 10 to 15 minutes before carving. Reserve the drippings in the pan.

Prepare the jus while it is resting. To serve, slice into ½ to 1-inch slices, spoon some jus onto each piece, and serve with fresh horseradish sauce.

Medium Rare=140°F; Medium = 145°F; medium well = 150°F; Well done=Please don't waste this beautiful piece of meat on well done!

Fresh Horseradish Sauce

Freshly grated horseradish is definitely worth it if you can find horseradish root as it has a much more full flavor than prepared horseradish. You can substitute prepared horseradish, but as the "heat" levels in it are generally higher, you may need to add it in increments. I like a very pungent horseradish sauce, but you may wish to use less or more fresh horseradish.

Makes 1½ cups

⅓ cup grated fresh horseradish, plus more for garnish

1 teaspoon minced garlic

1½ teaspoons Dijon mustard

¾ cup sour cream

½ teaspoon kosher salt

¼ teaspoon finely ground black pepper

Whisk all the ingredients together in a bowl. Store in the fridge, covered, for 2 to 3 hours, up to overnight, to allow the flavors to set. Taste for flavor, as horseradish may seem stronger after setting. Add more sour cream if necessary. I also like to sliver some extra horseradish and soak the slivers in water for 10 minutes to remove some of the bite. Remove from the water, drain, and dry with a paper towel, then garnish the prime rib with the raw horseradish slivers.

Quick Jus

This jus will pick up the smokiness from the prime rib by using some of the drippings. Instant flour (the main name brand is Wondra) is something I keep around as it is very easy to thicken sauces, soups, and gravies when they need that "little bit extra" but don't really need to cook longer. By using it in this recipe, you can gain 10 minutes of time it would take to get the proper consistency if you reduced the jus by simmering, which finishes this up just as your prime rib has rested enough!

Makes about 1½ cups

1 teaspoon olive oil

½ cup diced white onion

½ cup diced celery

½ cup diced carrot

1 cup beef stock

Drippings reserved from prime rib, fat poured off

1 teaspoon granulated garlic

1 teaspoon instant flour (preferably Wondra brand)

In a medium saucepan over high heat, combine the olive oil, onion, celery, and carrot and cook until the vegetables are browned, about 4 minutes. Pour in the beef stock and drippings. Scrape the bottom of the pan and cook for 2 minutes. Add the garlic and whisk. Sprinkle in the flour while whisking, bring to a boil, then decrease the heat to simmer for 5 to 10 minutes, until the jus has thickened slightly. Pour through a fine-mesh strainer and serve with the prime rib.

A good juicy burger topped with melted pimento and cheese makes for a good day. It's even better when you can add a lightly fried green tomato to give it a burst of tart freshness.

Serves 4

Deep South Burgers with Pimiento and Cheese and Fried Green Tomatoes

2 pounds ground beef

2 tablespoons Worcestershire sauce

1 teaspoon granulated garlic

1 teaspoon onion powder

2 tablespoons Grillin' Shake (page 22)

Pimiento and Cheese (recipe follows)

4 buns, for serving

Fried Green Tomatoes (page 96)

Prepare a medium-hot grill for cooking. In a bowl, combine the ground beef, Worcestershire, garlic, and onion powder. Stir until incorporated and pat into 4 (8-ounce) patties (I usually use a burger ring when I'm grilling so I can get evenly thick patties). Season both sides with the Grillin' Shake and place on a medium-hot grill. Cook to your desired temperature, about 4 to 5 minutes per side for medium to medium-well. As the burgers are nearing temperature, place 2 to 3 ounces of pimiento and cheese on each burger and let cook for 1 to 2 more minutes, or until the pimiento and cheese is beginning to melt. Place the burger patty on the bun with your favorite burger fixings, then top with a fried green tomato and enjoy.

continued

Pimiento and Cheese

This is my pimiento and cheese recipe when I'm looking for a "comfort sandwich." It makes for a pretty tasty burger topping as well!

Makes 4 cups

1 (8-ounce) package cream cheese, softened

½ cup mayonnaise

1 (4-ounce) jar diced pimientos, drained

2 teaspoons grated Vidalia or other sweet onion

½ teaspoon coarsely ground black pepper

½ teaspoon hot sauce, preferably Roasted Pepper Hot Sauce (page 29)

3 cups shredded cheddar cheese

¼ cup Candied Jalapeños, diced (page 47)

Salt

Whisk or beat the cream cheese until soft, then fold in the mayonnaise, pimientos, onion, pepper, hot sauce, cheese, and jalapeños. Stir until well mixed, then add salt if needed. Store, covered, in the refrigerator for up to a week, but bring to room temperature before using on burgers.

Fried Green Tomatoes

This is lightly breaded and cut thin to cook quickly and still have a fresh tomato texture.

Serves 4

Peanut oil, for frying

2 medium green tomatoes, cut into ¼ to ⅓-inch slices

1 cup buttermilk

1 cup self-rising flour

¼ cup white cornmeal

½ teaspoon salt

½ teaspoon freshly ground black pepper

Heat about 1 inch of peanut oil in a heavy skillet to 350°F. Place the tomato slices in a bowl and pour the buttermilk over them. On a plate, combine the flour, cornmeal, salt and pepper using a fork. Lightly dredge the tomato slices in the seasoned flour on both sides. Lay the tomatoes in the oil and cook until the bottom begins to brown, 2 to 3 minutes, then turn over to brown the other side for another 2 minutes. Transfer to a paper-towel-lined plate to drain until ready to serve.

THE ART OF TEXTURE AND TEMPERATURE

I am a texture person. I believe the texture of a product carries the flavors and allows it to express those flavors over the palate. A lot of very strong barbecue competitors will tell you "It's a texture contest, not a flavor contest." A properly cooked pork rib, for example, will have more flavor than a similarly seasoned but over- or undercooked one. However, texture is somewhat in the eye of the beholder. Witness chefs cringing when someone orders a well-done steak, as they feel the customer is ruining a great piece of meat. However, to the person ordering the well-done steak, that's the only way it's enjoyable. (Just ask my grandmother!)

When grilling, there are some fairly simple temperature guidelines to give you an idea of doneness. Steaks follow a simple progression from rare through well-done (see page 172), and chicken needs to achieve 165°F to be safe to consume. However, when we talk about long cook times, the exact temperature at which something is "done" can vary. "Hot and fast" barbecuers, of whom there are a growing number, cook meats to significantly higher internal temperatures than traditionalists. A pork butt cooked at 350°F for 4 hours may need to achieve 215+°F and rest for 3 to 4 hours to be "pulling texture," while one cooked at

225°F for 12 hours may have an internal temperature of only 175°F but be just as tender. Why is this? It has to do with breaking down the collagens in the meat and how long the internal temperature of the product stays in a zone high enough for the connective tissues, collagens, and fats to render and break down. A better way of showing this may be through an example of sous-vide cooking, where food is bagged and placed in water to be cooked. A piece of flank steak cooked in 130°F water for 12 to 14 hours will be as tender as a pulled pork sandwich, yet never cooked above 130°F. It's about the time AND temperature.

There are general guidelines on "perfect texture," regardless of how someone gets there. Brisket, for example, should maintain moisture, and the slices should hold together yet be tender enough to be pulled apart with a slight tug and have an easy chew. Ribs should never "fall off the bone," but you shouldn't have to gnaw on them either. There are variations of what constitutes "perfect texture" among many items, depending on regional preferences. A properly done rib in Memphis will probably be viewed as overcooked from someone from another part of the country (however, we're right and they're wrong).

Nature's way of showing us that we can accomplish anything is the beef brisket. If one can take an ornery, troublesome cut of meat like brisket and turn it into sublime, beefy goodness, you should be able to do anything you set your mind to! This recipe cuts down on the work of a brisket by using just the flat, a leaner, higher-yield section of the brisket. If you cook this, always look for at least a choice-grade brisket or higher to have a more tender, flavorful brisket. Allow around 7 hours to cook, although briskets sometimes dance to their own drummer where time is concerned. The injection is optional but will help amplify the beefy flavor. Also, in this recipe I call for spritzing apple juice on the brisket, which is also optional. I generally use water cookers, so the added moisture isn't necessary. However, cooks seem to love to check the meat and "do something" to it, and a little dab of apple juice certainly won't hurt. Similarly, wrapping in foil is optional. It will increase the cooking speed, maintain the color and moisture, but cost you some of the flavor. With flats, as they have less internal fat, I generally wrap them as I run a lot less chance of a dry brisket. In this recipe I use an 8-pound brisket flat. You may certainly use a smaller one (they are normally tighter trimmed), but keep a close eye on internal temperatures as it will cook more quickly than a whole packer brisket.

Serves 6 to 8

Beef Brisket Flat

BRISKET INJECTION

Makes about 2½ cups

3 cups beef stock

½ cup Worcestershire sauce

2 tablespoons granulated garlic

2 teaspoons onion powder

BRISKET

1 (7 to 8-pound) brisket flat, lightly trimmed of fat

2 tablespoons plus 1 teaspoon Basic "Memphis-Style" BBQ Rub (page 17), divided

2 tablespoons plus 1 teaspoon Cow Wow Rub (page 19), divided

1 cup apple juice, for spritzing (optional)

¼ cup BBQ Mother Sauce, Version 2 (page 24), for glazing

To make the brisket injection, bring the beef stock and Worcestershire to a boil in a small saucepan over medium heat, then decrease the heat to simmer. Whisk in the garlic and onion powder and continue to simmer until the stock has reduced by one-third. Remove from the heat and refrigerate until cool.

To prepare the brisket, in a small bowl mix 2 tablespoons each of the BBQ Rub and Cow Wow Rub together. Place the brisket in a pan just large enough to contain it, meat-side up. Using a meat injection needle, inject about 1 cup of the injection through the flat, using a checkerboard pattern (that is, inject every other inch all the way through the brisket) reserving the rest of the injection in the fridge until needed. Season the brisket thoroughly with the seasoning blend on both sides, about 2 tablespoons of seasoning per side. Return the brisket to the refrigerator, covered, for 4 hours, up to overnight. Remove from the fridge at least 30 minutes to 1 hour before cooking. Prepare a smoker or a grill for indirect heat (if using a grill or dry heat, add a water pan to the cooker) to cook at 250°F, using pecan or oak wood. Add 1 to 2 chunks of wood immediately when you put the brisket on and repeat as needed to keep the grill smoking until you wrap the meat. Place the brisket in the smoker, insert a meat thermometer into the thickest part of the brisket, and cook for around 4 hours, spritzing with apple juice every hour, if desired. When the internal temperature reaches around 150°F, remove the brisket and lay it on a large piece of heavy-duty aluminum foil. Combine the remaining teaspoon of each rub and sprinkle lightly on top of the brisket. Pour about 2 tablespoons of the reserved beef injection into the foil around the base of the brisket. Wrap tightly, return to the cooker, and reinsert a temperature probe.

Continue to cook, and as the meat approaches 202°F, begin to "test" by inserting a different temp probe into the meat. When it goes in "like butter," the brisket is done. This will probably be around 208°F, but each brisket is a little different. Set the wrapped brisket in a pan and open the foil for 3 or 4 minutes to "vent," then pour off the collected juices into a fat separator cup. Cover the brisket and put into a cooler (not with ice!) to rest for 1 to 2 hours. After the fat from the juice has risen, pour off the fat. Then pour the retained juices into the remaining 1½ cups of reserved beef injection and warm over low heat. Remove the brisket, place on a cutting board, and slice thinly across the grain. Dip several slices at a time into the reserved stock, then top lightly with BBQ Mother Sauce. Serve shingled on a plate with Ranch Beans (page 144) and Mexican Corn (page 141).

I do love tacos. I mean, really, really love tacos. Tacos are one of those items that can be as simple or as complicated as you want and be delicious either way. This marinade really brings a lot of fresh flavor components to the skirt steak, and although I like a tomatillo sauce, when you char them and add green tomatoes to the party it really starts to become addictive.

Makes 12 to 15 tacos

Skirt Steak Tacos with Charred Tomatillo-Green Tomato Sauce

MARINADE

½ medium yellow onion, diced

Leaves from ½ bunch cilantro, chopped

2 tablespoons peanut oil

2 tablespoons fresh lime juice

2 teaspoons kosher salt

1 tablespoon minced garlic

2 teaspoons coarsely ground black pepper

¼ teaspoon ancho chile powder

2 pounds skirt steak, trimmed

Warmed tortillas, for serving

CHARRED TOMATILLO AND GREEN TOMATO SAUCE

Makes about 5 cups, enough for tacos and dipping with chips!

1 tablespoon olive oil

3 medium green tomatoes (about 1 pound total), cored and cut in half

1 pound tomatillos, husked and rinsed

4 cloves garlic

2 teaspoons kosher salt

1 teaspoon coarsely ground black pepper

1 fresh jalapeño chile

¼ cup chopped cilantro leaves

½ teaspoon cumin seeds, toasted and ground

2 tablespoons honey

1 teaspoon minced fresh oregano

½ cup fresh corn kernels

½ cup diced red onion

Peanut oil for the grates

Warmed 6-inch tortillas, for serving

continued

To prepare the beef, in a mixing bowl combine the onion, cilantro, oil, lime juice, salt, garlic, black pepper, and chile powder. Stir well, then pour into a resealable plastic bag and add the skirt steak. Place in the fridge to marinate for at least 8 hours and up to 24 hours, turning occasionally.

To make the sauce, lightly oil the tomatillos and tomatoes with olive oil, then place on a hot grill until charred but not blackened. Rotate around to get the grill effect on all sides. Roughly chop the green tomatoes and tomatillos and add to a bowl. Mince the garlic and add to the bowl along with the salt and pepper. Clean, stem, and dice the jalapeño, removing the seeds if desired, then add to the bowl. Add the cilantro, cumin, honey, and oregano and pour into a blender and pulse a couple of times, then purée for 15 seconds. Stir in the corn and red onion. Set aside until ready to serve.

When ready to cook, remove the steaks from the marinade and shake off any excess. Discard the marinade. Using peanut oil or another high-smoke-point oil, oil the grill grates and prepare the grill to cook at hot temperature with wood chunks (or a smoker box in a gas grill). Lay the skirt steaks down and cook for 2 to 3 minutes, until grill marks form and the steak releases. Turn over and cook for 2½ minutes for medium-rare, 3 to 4 minutes for medium. Remove from the grill and rest for 5 minutes (remember, skirt steaks are thin and cook fast and will come up a few degrees while resting). Cut into strips against the grain and serve with warmed tortillas and tomatillo and green tomato sauce.

I love steak so much I use everyday events as a justification to "reward" myself with one. Got dressed? Good job, have a steak. Picked up dry cleaning? Awesome! Have a steak. See, it's not hard when you put your mind to it. Strip steaks fall into the tenderness zone between sirloins and ribeyes but maintain a good beefy flavor. Onions cooked on the grill along with the steaks amplify the grill flavor with your meal. These have a beautiful look as well with a light balsamic glaze. The steak rub for this recipe gives the steak a bit of au poivre effect.

Serves 4

New York Strip with Balsamic Sweet Onions

BALSAMIC ONION FLOWERS

4 medium sweet onions

¼ cup olive oil

2 tablespoons balsamic vinegar

2 tablespoons Grilled Steak Seasoning (page 22)

NEW YORK STRIP

4 (12-ounce) New York strip steaks

1½ teaspoons olive oil

2 tablespoons Grilled Steak Seasoning (page 22)

To make the flowers, peel the onions, then thinly slice off the stem end of each onion and barely slice the root end flat so the onion will stand up. Use an apple corer and cut three-quarters of the way through. Place the onions in a small aluminum foil pan, whisk the olive oil and balsamic together, and then brush over the tops. Place on a grill set for indirect heat and cook for 40 to 50 minutes, until tender and the "leaves" have opened. Lightly sprinkle with the steak seasoning before serving.

To make the strip steaks, lightly brush both sides of the steaks with olive oil, then season with the steak seasoning on both sides. Let come up to room temperature at least 30 minutes before grilling. Prepare a medium-hot grill with some pecan wood or similar. Place the steaks on the grill and cook for 3 minutes, then rotate a quarter turn and cook for another 2 to 3 minutes. Flip the steaks and repeat. Remove from the grill and let rest, covered lightly with foil, for 5 minutes. Six minutes per side should yield medium-rare to medium steaks; adjust the cooking time for your preference and the thickness of the steak. Serve with the onion flowers.

Beef back ribs never get the credit they're due, especially around the pork-centric area where I reside. Part of the reason they are underused is the butchering process—sometimes the meat packers scrape off too much meat, but mainly just because they are not common in the South. The cooking process resembles that of its porcine counterparts, pork back ribs, and generates wonderfully tender and delicious meat. You will need a lot more weight per person than you think, as the fat renders and the meat shrinks down. Look for slabs with the most meat on them when shopping.

Serves 4

Beef Back Ribs

2 slabs beef back ribs (7 to 8
   pounds total)

1 tablespoon yellow mustard

¼ cup Cow Wow Rub (page 19),
   divided

½ cup beef stock

¼ cup Dr. Pepper BBQ Sauce
   (page 27), for glazing, plus more
   for dipping

Open the ribs and place bone side up. Slide the tip of a spoon between a bone and the membrane that is over the bones. Using a paper towel to grip, pull the membrane off entirely and discard. Trim any large fat deposits, but most will render during the cooking process, so it is acceptable to leave them. Sprinkle each side of the ribs with about 1½ teaspoons of the rub, then slather mustard over them and rub them thoroughly to coat. Store in a pan in the fridge for at least 2 hours, up to overnight to marinate (if longer than a couple of hours, I cover the pan with foil).

Remove from the fridge about 30 minutes before cooking and sprinkle with another 1½ teaspoons of rub on each side and let them sit out to come up to room temperature. Prepare a smoker to cook at 225°F with a bolder wood, such as pecan. Place the ribs in the smoker meat side up and cook for 2 hours. Raise the temperature to 250°F, wrap the ribs in aluminum foil, pour in the beef stock, and continue to cook for an additional 2 hours, until the meat is tender and fats are rendered. Lightly glaze with BBQ sauce and let rest for 5 minutes before serving.

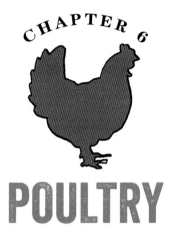

POULTRY

When in doubt for what to cook, many of us go with the old standby, chicken or other poultry. However, chicken for dinner doesn't have to mean another dry, bland chicken breast; when cooked and seasoned properly, it can be wonderful. Poultry has so many varieties and is so conducive to any cooking style that it has rightfully earned its place as a dinner mainstay.

Some poultry isn't blessed with an intrinsically unique flavor; chicken, for instance, is an inherently neutral canvas. Use that to paint it with a little smoke, some char, some bold spices, or a fresh sauce, and you have something worthy of a special dinner. Other poultry shares some of the same attributes as chicken but may have more flavor for you to take advantage of. Ducks and doves, being dark meat, can have much richer flavors and respond well to more robust sauces or marinades. Turkey is one of my favorites, and I stock up on whole turkeys and turkey breasts during the holidays and cook them through the year. My Smoked Peppered Turkey Waffle Sandwich is really just an excuse for me to cook more turkey. I'm a firm believer that all of these beautiful spices, herbs, and seasonings are on this planet to enjoy and make our lives, and meals, a little bit more exciting. Enjoy the journey!

Smoked chicken is a wonderful thing. By smoking it, you get a much different texture than when roasting, as well as the benefit of a nice smoky flavor. I think smoked chicken should be done simply and with a lighter fruitwood such as apple or with a medium-bold wood such as pecan. Many times if I have room on a smoker, I will smoke a chicken so I will be able to make Smoked Chicken Salad (page 110) or Smoked Chicken and Wild Rice Soup (page 112). Sometimes enough extra chicken just doesn't get saved after dinner, so make extra!

Serves 2 to 4

Smoked Chicken

1 (4 to 5-pound) whole chicken, giblets removed, excess fat trimmed

1 teaspoon olive oil

2 tablespoons Basic "Memphis-Style" BBQ Rub (page 17)

Prepare a smoker to cook at 250°F. I much prefer to smoke chicken in either halves or spatchcock style, as it allows the chicken to cook more evenly. To spatchcock, simply cut out the backbone with a pair of kitchen shears, fold the chicken open, and press down lightly to flatten slightly. Lightly oil the skin with olive oil and generously sprinkle both sides of the chicken with the BBQ Rub. Place in the smoker skin-side up and cook for 1 hour and 45 minutes, until the breast registers 165°F and the thigh 175°F. Remove and rest for 5 to 10 minutes, then cut into serving pieces (allow a quarter- to a half-chicken per person) or let cool to room temperature and pull the meat off the bones if using for recipes like the chicken salad that follows.

MELISSA'S TIP

I learned to barbecue the old-fashioned way: by time, temperature, and feel. You learn to know when meat is done by looking and touching, and your index finger becomes your best temperature gauge. However, chicken and poultry are a different matter. The difference between cooking the chicken by feel—removing it from the cooker so that it will finish right above the safety zone of 165°F—and perhaps overcooking it because you were guessing is the difference between "Great dinner!" and "Well, thanks for cooking." Use a thermometer, preferably an instant-read or very fast electronic one. I use them, and they definitely help.

First, I really like saying "Brick Chicken." Second, grilling chicken this way will speed up the cooking process as well as get crispier skin—always good things. The way to go about this dish is to start the gravy and rice ahead of time and then grill the chicken, even though it is a whole chicken and will cook rather quickly. You will get some char on this, so you don't want to leave it and spend time doing something else while it cooks.

The gravy is flavored by one of my all-time favorite ingredients, tasso ham. Tasso is rather hard to come by outside of Louisiana. If you don't have tasso, substitute regular ham plus one tablespoon of your favorite Cajun seasoning. You can also go more traditional with the dirty rice here by substituting chicken livers or giblets for the sausage. (Cook by simmering for 30 minutes covered in water, then cool, chop, and add to the rice.)

Serves 4

Brick Chicken with Tasso Gravy and Dirty Rice

TASSO GRAVY

Makes 2 cups

4 tablespoons (½ stick) unsalted butter

¼ cup diced yellow onion

¼ cup diced celery

¼ cup diced green bell pepper

1 bay leaf

¾ cup diced tasso ham

½ teaspoon cayenne

1 tablespoon minced garlic

¼ cup all-purpose flour

1 cup chicken stock

1 teaspoon kosher salt

1 teaspoon freshly ground black pepper

DIRTY RICE

1 cup rice

2 cups chicken stock

8 ounces pork sausage

1 cup diced white onion

1 cup diced green bell pepper

2 bay leaves

2 cloves garlic, minced

Salt and freshly ground black pepper

Scallions, chopped, for garnish

BRICK CHICKEN

½ cup olive oil

⅓ cup freshly squeezed lemon juice

3 cloves garlic, minced

1 teaspoon minced fresh thyme leaves

1 (4 to 5-pound) whole chicken

1½ teaspoons kosher salt

1 teaspoon coarsely ground black pepper

1 brick, wrapped in foil

Smokin' Hot in the South

To make the gravy, place the butter in a skillet over medium-high heat. Add the onion, celery, bell pepper, and bay leaf and cook for 4 minutes, until they begin to soften. Add the ham, cayenne, and garlic and continue to cook for 4 minutes. With a slotted spoon, remove the ham and vegetables, then add the flour and whisk until the flour is browned, 4 to 5 minutes. Begin to add the chicken stock in small increments while whisking. After you have incorporated all the chicken stock, add the vegetables back in and stir. Season with salt and pepper. If the gravy is too thick, it may be thinned with water, 1 tablespoon at a time.

To make the rice, place the rice and chicken stock in a pot and bring to a boil, then cover and cook for 20 minutes, until the rice is done. Remove from the heat.

In another skillet over medium-high heat, cook the pork sausage until browned. Remove the sausage from the skillet, leaving 1 to 2 tablespoons of rendered fat in the skillet. Add the onion, pepper, and bay leaves and cook for 3 minutes, then add the garlic and continue to cook until soft, about 10 minutes. Add the sausage and rice back to the skillet and turn the heat to low. Stir the mixture and add salt and pepper to taste. (This will depend on the type of sausage you use.) Garnish with scallions.

To make the chicken, place a cast-iron skillet on a grill and preheat the grill to medium-hot.

In a small bowl, whisk the olive oil, lemon juice, garlic, and thyme and set aside. Using kitchen shears, cut the backbone from the chicken. Using a brush, coat the chicken on both sides with the olive oil mix, then season with salt and pepper.

Place the chicken on the grill, skin-side up, and place the heated cast-iron skillet on top of the chicken. Place a brick in the cast-iron skillet to help weigh it down. Cook for 8 to 10 minutes. Remove the skillet and flip the chicken, then replace the skillet and brick. Cook for another 8 to 10 minutes, until an instant-read thermometer reads 175°F in the thigh area.

Remove the chicken from the grill and let it rest, loosely covered, for 5 to 10 minutes. Cut the chicken into quarters and serve over the rice, topped with gravy.

Chicken salad has long been a mainstay of the "church social" or "afternoon tea," many times in the form of finger sandwiches. If you go door to door, you will get as many different recipes and methods for chicken salad as doors you knock on. If you look at several of the recipes, you will soon realize that the correct "chicken salad" is in the eye of the chef making it that day. It's a remarkably versatile dish and can take any number of different ingredients/methods and still be delicious. When I make chicken salad, I love the subtle flavor that smoked chicken brings to the party, along with the texture of walnuts and the sweet pop of grapes, so I've included them in my recipe.

Serves 4 to 6

Smoked Chicken Salad

1 pound pulled smoked chicken

1 cup mayonnaise

1 cup halved seedless red grapes

½ cup diced sweet gherkin pickles, plus 2 tablespoons pickle juice

⅓ cup finely diced celery

¼ cup finely diced white onion

¼ cup chopped walnuts

¾ teaspoon kosher salt

¾ teaspoon coarsely ground black pepper

In a large mixing bowl, fold all the ingredients together to incorporate without breaking apart the chicken too much. Serve over butter lettuce with sliced fresh tomatoes and strawberries for a cool salad or on sliced pumpernickel or wheat bread as a sandwich.

This is a great use for any chicken you may have left over from the Smoked Chicken recipe (page 107). This is one of my favorite meals when fall finally comes after the South's long hot summer. In a pinch, pulled rotisserie chicken will do just fine, but you'll lose some of the smoky nuance of the soup.

Makes about 2 quarts

Smoked Chicken and Wild Rice Soup

1 cup raw wild rice (not parcooked)

6 cups chicken stock, divided

6 tablespoons unsalted butter, divided

1 medium yellow onion, diced (about 1 cup)

½ cup diced carrots

1 cup diced celery

1 tablespoon minced garlic

2 bay leaves

1 teaspoon salt, plus more as needed

1 teaspoon freshly ground black pepper, plus more as needed

½ cup flour

1 cup milk

2 cups pulled Smoked Chicken (page 107)

1 teaspoon sage

½ teaspoon fresh thyme

½ cup heavy cream

In a small stockpot, bring the wild rice and 1½ cups of the chicken stock to a boil, stir, and then cover and lower the heat. Simmer for 15 minutes, then remove from the heat and let stand for 5 to 10 minutes.

In another stockpot over medium-high heat, cook 1 tablespoon of the butter, the onion, carrots, celery, garlic, bay leaves, salt, and pepper until the vegetables are softened, then add the remaining 5 tablespoons of butter. After the butter is melted, add the flour in small increments while whisking. After all the flour has been added, continue to stir for 3 to 4 minutes to cook out the raw flour flavor. Lower the heat to medium, then pour the milk in slowly while whisking to incorporate. Continue to cook and add in the remaining 4½ cups chicken stock, the chicken, sage, thyme, and cream and simmer for 10 minutes. Add the cooked rice, stir, and season with salt and pepper to taste.

This will probably be the longest time you've ever taken to make a sandwich, but since you'll be smoking the turkey breast yourself, it will definitely be worth it! The waffle recipe makes waffles from scratch that seem to hold up to being made into a sandwich a little bit better than a purchased mix, but that will be fine if you prefer. (Try even putting a hamburger bun in the waffle iron; the magic comes from the added crispness the waffle iron will impart, although it sure is fun eating a sandwich on an actual waffle.) To dress the sandwich, I love adding some of my Chipotle Aioli (page 30), a slice of provolone, some fresh arugula, and a nice slice of a vine-ripened tomato, but fixin's are strictly optional—use your faves! Absolutely satisfying!

I've tried making sweet potato chips many ways, and two things stand out in my tests: One, use a mandoline and cut the sweet potatoes very thin, and two, find narrow sweet potatoes, as that makes them easier to slice. When I serve these with a turkey sandwich, I like to toss them with some chopped fresh rosemary and Smoked Sea Salt (page 28), but you can use whatever herb you think will go with your meal or just have them as a snack.

Makes 4 sandwiches, plus more turkey (and waffle buns) for snacking!

Smoked Pepper Turkey Waffle Sandwich with Sweet Potato Chips

SMOKED PEPPER TURKEY

1 (5 to 7-pound) bone-in turkey breast

1 teaspoon extra virgin olive oil

2 tablespoons Pepper Poultry Rub (page 18)

4 sprigs fresh thyme

3 to 4 sprigs fresh rosemary

2 to 3 sprigs fresh sage

WAFFLE BUNS

Makes 12 medium waffles (enough for 6 sandwiches)

4 cups all-purpose flour

1 teaspoon kosher salt

1 teaspoon coarsely ground black pepper

½ teaspoon finely chopped fresh rosemary

2 tablespoons plus 1 teaspoon baking powder

¼ cup sugar

2 eggs, lightly whisked

3 cups milk, at room temperature

⅔ cup melted unsalted butter (10⅔ tablespoons)

1 teaspoon flaked sea salt

SWEET POTATO CHIPS

Makes 2 to 3 cups, depending on size

2 sweet potatoes, peeled

½ cup peanut oil

1 tablespoon chopped fresh rosemary

1 teaspoon Smoked Sea Salt (page 28)

1 teaspoon coarsely ground black pepper

continued

To make the turkey, prepare a smoker to cook at 250°F with apple or another fruit wood.

Rinse the turkey and pat it dry. Brush it with the olive oil, then generously season all surfaces of the turkey with the Pepper Poultry Rub. Place a strip of aluminum foil just larger than the turkey in the smoker, lay the herbs on it, and place the turkey, breast-bone-side down, on top of the herbs. Smoke for 3½ hours, until the internal temperature in the thickest part of the breast reaches 165°F. Remove the turkey from the smoker (including the foil with the herbs) and set it on a larger piece of foil. Wrap tightly for 20 to 30 minutes to rest.

Wearing gloves, remove the turkey from the foil and fillet the breasts from the bones. Slice thinly for sandwiches.

To make the waffle buns, spray a waffle iron with nonstick cooking spray and preheat it.

In a large bowl, mix the flour, kosher salt, pepper, rosemary, baking powder, and sugar. In a separate bowl, whisk the eggs, then stir in the milk and melted butter. Add the egg mixture to the dry ingredients and stir until all the flour is incorporated. Ladle the batter into the waffle iron. Cook until crisp, then remove. Sprinkle the top waffle bun with flaked sea salt. Repeat with the remaining batter.

To make the sweet potato chips, using a mandoline, slice the sweet potatoes very thinly and set aside. In a large frying pan, heat the oil to 350°F. Lay the chips in the oil, but do not overcrowd. Cook for 2 to 3 minutes, then turn the chips over and cook until crisp but not burned, about 2 to 3 minutes. Transfer to a paper-towel-lined plate to drain and cool. Sprinkle with the rosemary, Smoked Sea Salt, and black pepper.

MELISSA'S
TIP

To brine or not to brine: That is the question. Generally speaking, I believe brining can add some moisture and flavor to meats, especially poultry. While there are times I do like to brine, most of the time for turkey I prefer a flavorful rub, complementary smoke, and monitoring the temperature to pull the turkey at just the right time to ensure a juicy bird.

Begin cooking the collard greens first, as they will take at least an hour to cook. As with any greens, look for smaller ones, which will be younger and more tender. Try to avoid the bags of prewashed and cut greens, as generally I find they are not the best quality. Collard greens are rather pungent, so whenever possible I cook them on a side burner outside. Collards are traditionally seasoned with smoked ham hock, but I prefer to use bacon since it distributes more evenly through the greens.

If using wild duck breasts, soak the breasts in some salted ice water for about an hour, then drain and pat them dry before grilling. This will help pull out some of the gaminess of the wild duck.

Serves 4

Grilled Duck Breast and Collard Greens with Bacon

COLLARD GREENS WITH BACON

2 pounds collard greens

1 tablespoon peanut oil

5 slices bacon, cut into pieces

1 cup chopped white onion

1 tablespoon minced garlic

1 tablespoon kosher salt

½ tablespoon freshly ground black pepper

6 cups chicken stock

GRILLED DUCK BREAST

4 (5 to 6-ounce) individual boneless duck breasts

1 teaspoon kosher salt

2 teaspoons coarsely ground black pepper

1 tablespoon butter

1 small white onion, julienne cut

2 Granny Smith apples, peeled, cored, julienne cut, and covered with lemon juice

1 teaspoon Dijon mustard

½ cup cider vinegar

1 tablespoon finely chopped fresh flat-leaf parsley

1 tablespoon light brown sugar

Smoked Sea Salt (page 28)

To make the greens, wash them thoroughly and cut them into 2 to 3-inch pieces. Heat the oil in a medium stockpot over medium-high heat. Add the bacon and cook it until crisp. Add the onion and cook for 3 to 4 minutes, then add the garlic and continue to cook until the garlic is golden. Add the collard greens and cook for 2 to 3 minutes, until they begin to wilt. Season with salt and pepper and add the chicken stock. Decrease the heat to low and simmer for 45 minutes to 1 hour, depending on the age of the greens.

To make the duck breasts, set up a grill for 2-zone cooking, with 1 side hot and the other medium.

Using a sharp knife, score the fat on the breasts in a diamond shape, taking care not to cut into the meat. Season both sides of each breast with salt and pepper. Place a well-seasoned cast-iron skillet on the hot side of the grill and allow to heat. Add the butter, allow it to melt, and place the breasts skin-side down in the skillet. Cook the breasts for 5 minutes, sliding the pan to the cool side if they're cooking too quickly, then take them out of the pan and lay them on the grill on the uncooked side for 3 to 4 minutes, depending on the desired doneness. When ready, remove the breasts from the grill, plate, and loosely cover with foil to rest.

Spoon off any excess duck fat in the pan (leaving approximately 2 tablespoons) and move the skillet back to the high-temperature side (or move to a burner). Add the onion and cook for 2 minutes, then add the apples and allow them to brown as you stir, 2 to 3 minutes. Add the mustard, vinegar, parsley, and brown sugar and stir until the brown sugar is dissolved. Remove from the heat.

To plate, place a serving of greens on a plate using tongs and allowing the excess liquid to drip off the greens. Cut the duck breasts on the bias, then shingle over the greens. Spoon the onion-apple mix over the duck breasts, then sprinkle lightly with the Smoked Sea Salt.

OK, I will admit this isn't the healthiest way to cook a chicken breast. So just decide to eat a salad or something tomorrow, and enjoy these today. See? All the guilt is gone. The stuffing in these breasts really isn't the important thing; feel free to experiment and put your favorite items in there. When checking the internal temperature, make sure the probe is in the chicken, not the stuffing, so you can get an accurate reading.

Serves 4

Smoked Chicken Bacon Bombs

4 (6-ounce) boneless, skinless chicken breasts

1 cup shredded mozzarella cheese

4 slices bacon, cooked and chopped, plus 8 slices, uncooked, divided

1 teaspoon minced jalapeño chile

1 tablespoon minced red bell pepper

½ teaspoon minced garlic

2 tablespoons Pepper Poultry Rub (page 18)

1 cup chopped fresh spinach

2 teaspoons Grillin' Shake (page 22)

½ cup BBQ Mother Sauce, Version 2 (page 24), plus more for dipping

Set up a grill for indirect heat to cook at 275°F with apple wood. Place a sheet of plastic wrap over each chicken breast (to help with the mess) and, using a mallet, pound the breasts to ¼-inch thickness. In a small bowl, mix the cheese, cooked bacon bits, jalapeño, bell pepper, and garlic. Season both sides of the breasts with the rub, then lay them flat, smooth-side down, and place a quarter of the spinach on each breast and sprinkle a quarter of the cheese mixture over each, leaving a ½-inch edge. Roll each breast up jelly-roll style, as tightly as possible, then wrap 2 raw bacon slices around each breast and secure with toothpicks. Lightly sprinkle the rolled breasts with Grillin' Shake and place on the grill. Smoke for 1 hour, until the internal temperature of the chicken reaches 150°F, then place them on the direct side of the grill to finish cooking and sear the bacon. Roll the breasts over until the bacon is browned on all sides and the breasts' internal temperature is over 160°F. Move them back to the cooler side of the grill and glaze the breasts with BBQ Mother Sauce; let them set for 5 minutes. Remove from the grill and serve, with extra sauce on the side.

This brine works well on just about any poultry, although brining times may vary depending on the size of the bird. This brine adds a nice flavor to the chicken as well as helping with moisture, and the rotisserie gives that crisp skin that I like.

Serves 2 to 4

Hard Cider-Brined Rotisserie Chicken

HARD CIDER BRINE

8 cups water, divided

1 cup kosher salt

½ cup sugar

½ cup cider vinegar

½ cup honey

1 teaspoon cumin seeds

1 teaspoon mustard seeds

4 cloves garlic, smashed

2 sprigs fresh rosemary

1 tablespoon minced fresh sage

2 cups ice

3 (12-ounce) bottles hard pear cider (apple cider will do if you can't find pear)

ROTISSERIE CHICKEN

1 (4 to 5-pound) whole chicken

2 tablespoons Basic "Memphis-Style" BBQ Rub (page 17) or Pepper Poultry Rub (page 18)

To make the brine, heat 4 cups of the water in a saucepot and add the salt, sugar, and vinegar and bring to a boil; stir to dissolve the sugar and salt. Decrease the heat and add the honey, cumin, mustard, garlic, rosemary, and sage. Stir, then remove from the heat. Pour the mixture in a nonreactive container (plastic, glass, etc.) large enough to contain the chicken and brine. Add the remaining 4 cups of water, ice, and cider. Place in the refrigerator to cool. Once the brine is cooled, immerse the chicken, laying a plate over it to keep it under the brine, and put it back in the fridge. Brine the chicken for a minimum of 4 hours, up to 12 hours for the full flavor effect.

Generally, rotisserie equipped grills have a minimum of three grill burners, plus many are equipped with a "rotisserie burner" mounted in the back of the grill. When cooking on a gas rotisserie, I leave the middle burner off to lessen the risk of flame-ups (especially with chicken) and only use the back burner during the last few minutes to help crisp the skin. Prepare the grill to cook around 400°F using the two end burners, leaving any back or rotisserie burners off. (I also place a small aluminum pan there to catch drippings and make clean up easier.) Season the chicken with rub, sprinkling it inside as well as outside. Secure the chicken to the spit and turn on the rotisserie motor. Cook for 45 minutes to 1 hour (depending on the size of the chicken) and check the temperature. It should be in the 155 to 160°F range in the thigh. Turn on the rear burner (if equipped) to a medium-low to medium range to help finish the chicken and crisp the skin. Continue to cook until the chicken is golden, its thigh temperature reads 165 to 170°F, and its breast temperature reads 160 to 165°F. (After turning on the back burner, it should take about 10 to 15 more minutes to finish the chicken, if not using one.) Turn off all the burners, carefully remove, and rest, lightly covered in foil, for 10 to 15 minutes, and carve.

Every September my stepfather, George, would go dove hunting. I think hunting is rather a misnomer, as basically the men would stand in a field and shoot at doves that happened to fly over their position. If this sounds rather one-sided, it's not—most of the time the doves won. However, George usually would come back with a few dove breasts, which he would marinate and grill. Dove breasts are dark meat, but they don't have the gaminess of some wild fowl.

Serves 3 to 4

Smoked Dove Breasts

12 (3 to 4-ounce) dove breasts

1 cup Italian dressing

1 cup good red wine

2 jalapeños, seeded, and cut into strips

6 slices bacon, cut in half

2 teaspoons Grillin' Shake (page 22)

¼ cup BBQ Mother Sauce, Version 2 (page 24), for glazing

Remove any excess fat from the dove breasts, then place them in a pan and pour the Italian dressing and wine over them; marinate for at least 8 hours, or overnight.

Remove the breasts from the marinade and shake off any excess. Discard the marinade. Lay 2 strips of the jalapeño on each breast and wrap bacon around the breast, securing it with a toothpick. Lightly season the bacon and breasts with Grillin' Shake.

Prepare a smoker to cook at 275°F, with oak or pecan wood. Place the breasts in the smoker for 35 minutes, until the bacon crisps. Lightly glaze with BBQ Sauce and cook for 10 minutes more to tighten the sauce, then remove and serve.

This is a super quick yet tasty item to serve. I generally go with the seasons on the sauce, as you can substitute herbs such as sage, rosemary, tarragon, or cilantro depending on your mood and the time of year.

Serves 4

Grilled Chicken Breast with Basil Cream Gravy

GRILLED CHICKEN BREAST

4 (6-ounce) boneless, skinless chicken breasts

2½ teaspoons olive oil, divided

2 tablespoons Fresh Herb Rub (page 20)

BASIL CREAM GRAVY

3 tablespoons olive oil

1 cup thinly sliced baby bella mushrooms

3 tablespoons unsalted butter

1 tablespoon minced garlic

1 teaspoon salt

¼ teaspoon finely ground black pepper

¾ cup heavy cream

1 teaspoon instant flour, preferably Wondra brand

1½ tablespoons diced fresh basil

To make the chicken, preheat a grill to medium-hot and place a griddle or cast-iron skillet on the grill. Trim the breasts of any excess fat. Lightly pound them to get a more even thickness. Brush the breasts with 1 teaspoon of the olive oil, then season them on all sides with the Fresh Herb Rub. Let the breasts sit out for 15 to 20 minutes to come to room temperature, then place them, smooth-side down, on the skillet after warming the remaining 1½ teaspoons oil in it. Cook about 6 minutes, then flip each breast over and cook 5 to 6 minutes more, until the internal temperature reaches 163°F, ensuring it rises above 165°F before serving. Remove from the grill, lightly cover on a plate, and let rest for 5 minutes.

To make the gravy, heat the oil in a small saucepan over medium heat. Add the mushrooms and cook for 4 to 5 minutes, until soft. Add and melt the butter, then add the garlic, salt, and pepper and cook for 2 minutes. Stir in the cream and allow it to heat, then sprinkle the flour over the gravy while stirring to keep it from forming lumps. Bring to a light boil, then decrease the heat to low, stir in the basil and hold while waiting on the chicken, stirring occasionally.

SEAFOOD

I have always loved the smell of the ocean and the relaxation that comes from the sights and sounds of the waves gently rolling in to the beach. It has never hurt that in some of our local seafood houses you can eat some of the freshest, most expertly prepared local seafood, many times caught within hours of your meal.

A drive along the Gulf Coast is really a remarkable experience. You will see the bayous and sugar sands, the seafood shacks and the tourist traps. Concentrate on the local dives, the places off the beaten path and the true "old towns" and you will be rewarded by mingling with some of the most down-to-earth, friendly people in the nation. The fact that they can usually cook some of the best seafood imaginable is a pretty nice feather in their caps as well!

This chapter is about cooking fresh seafood, whether it's a crab cake cooked on a plank or scallops cooked on the grill. I try to treat the seafood carefully and accentuate it with flavors that are complementary. Generally seafood will benefit from just a brief hint of smoke, and the proteins will not hold up to a longer cooking process, so these items are best prepared on a hot to medium-hot grill with quick cooking techniques.

It's not hard to talk me into a crab cake, especially these! These aren't your normal heavily breaded crab cakes. The crab is really the star in this recipe, which is one reason I splurge to get the jumbo lump crabmeat when I'm making these.

Makes 8 crab cakes

Plank-Fired Crab Cakes

¼ cup mayonnaise

1 tablespoon whole-grain mustard

1 teaspoon fresh lemon juice

½ teaspoon kosher salt

½ teaspoon freshly ground black pepper

1 tablespoon fresh flat-leaf parsley

1 tablespoon finely chopped scallion (green and white parts)

1 pound jumbo lump crabmeat

⅓ cup panko bread crumbs

2 cedar planks (or other wood), soaked in water for 1 hour

1 tablespoon melted butter

1½ teaspoons Blackening Seasoning (page 18)

Mississippi Comeback Sauce (page 27), for serving

Combine the mayonnaise, mustard, lemon juice, salt, pepper, parsley, and scallion in a medium mixing bowl. Add the crab and panko, gently folding both in so as to break up the crab as little as possible while still incorporating everything. Refrigerate the mixture for 30 minutes.

Heat a grill to hot, approximately 500° to 600°F. Place the planks on the grill for 2 minutes, then flip them, leaving for another minute. Remove the planks from the grill.

Form the crab mixture into 4 mounds on each plank (you can use a ½-cup measuring cup to give you an idea of the right size), pressing down on each slightly but not so much as to break up the crab pieces. Brush with melted butter and lightly sprinkle each with the seasoning.

Place the planks back on the grill and cook for 5 to 8 minutes, until the crab cakes are hot and slightly browned. Remove the planks from the grill and use a thin metal spatula to carefully remove the crab cakes from the plank and plate. Serve with the sauce on the side.

The humble, homely-looking catfish has long been a staple on Southern tables. When I was growing up, I would spend many a day fishing for catfish, then enjoying the fruits of my labor for dinner. Mississippi farm-raised catfish have been a great development since my younger years, as you can now get clean-tasting, sustainably raised catfish without having to get your fishing pole ready. You do have to be careful when grilling it, as it can stick and tear, so make sure you oil your grates in addition to the fish. Fried Hominy will give you a nice texture contrast and is wonderfully addictive. For the best results on this dish, prepare and fry the hominy ahead of time, then set aside or hold it in a warming oven. Make the sauce and hold on low heat, or make ahead, refrigerate, and heat up as needed. Start the rice a few minutes before grilling the catfish and serve warm.

Serves 4

"BBQ" Catfish with Creamy Corn Sauce and Fried Hominy

FRIED HOMINY

1 (14-ounce) can hominy

½ cup all-purpose flour

¼ cup cornstarch

2 teaspoons Basic "Memphis-Style" BBQ Rub (page 17), divided

Peanut oil, for frying

CATFISH

4 (6 to 8-ounce) boneless, skinless farm-raised catfish fillets

¼ cup peanut oil, plus more for oiling the grill

¼ cup Basic "Memphis-Style" BBQ Rub (page 17)

2 cups cooked white or brown rice

2 tablespoons diced scallion (green and white parts), for garnish

2 cups cooked white rice

CREAMY CORN SAUCE

1 tablespoon peanut oil

½ cup minced celery

¼ cup minced green bell pepper

¼ cup minced red bell pepper

1 tablespoon minced garlic

1 teaspoon salt

½ teaspoon coarsely ground black pepper

2½ cups heavy cream

1 cup fresh-cut corn kernels

½ teaspoon chopped fresh oregano leaves

1 teaspoon chopped fresh flat-leaf parsley

To make the hominy, drain the hominy and spread it out on paper towels. Put the hominy on a sheet pan and place in the refrigerator for 2 to 4 hours to dry.

The catfish is best prepared on a gas grill with a smoker box or on a charcoal grill with some wood chunks/chips to give it a hint of smoke. Prepare a medium-hot grill. Brush the catfish with the oil, then season both sides of the fillets thoroughly and pat the seasoning onto the fillets. Place the fillets on the grill "skin"-side down for 3 to 4 minutes, or until fillet "releases" from the grill and can be turned over. Gently turn them over and cook for another 3 to 4 minutes. Test for doneness by lightly pressing with your finger. The fillet should feel firm but not dry. Remove the fillets from the grill.

To make the corn sauce, in a medium nonstick skillet over medium-high heat, heat the oil and the add celery and both bell peppers. Cook for 2 minutes, until the celery and bell peppers soften. Add the garlic, salt, and pepper and cook for 1 to 2 minutes, until the garlic is golden. Add the heavy cream and corn, stir, and decrease the heat to medium-low to simmer for 8 to 10 minutes, until the cream has thickened, whisking often to keep the cream from sticking. Stir in the oregano and parsley and serve.

Mix the flour, cornstarch, and 1 teaspoon of the BBQ rub together, then add the hominy and toss to coat. Place the hominy kernels in a strainer to shake off any excess breading mix.

Heat the oil in a small frying pan, 2 tablespoons at a time, until it is around 350°F. Add the hominy in batches and fry for 4 to 6 minutes, stirring occasionally, until the breading has crisped. Remove the cooked hominy from the skillet and place on a paper towel–lined plate and sprinkle lightly with the remaining 1 teaspoon of BBQ rub.

To serve, lay ½ cup of rice on a plate and shingle a catfish fillet over it. Spoon the corn sauce over the catfish, top the sauce with a pinch of scallion, and sprinkle the hominy around the plate.

Soft-shell crabs always make for a wonderful presentation. Generally in the South, I see them offered fried (well, who am I kidding, everything down here is usually offered fried!), but I love to grill them and top them with a rich lemon beurre blanc. Grit cakes are a great use for some leftover grits and provide a nice texture contrast.

Serves 4

Grilled Soft-Shell Crabs with Stone-Ground Grit Cakes and Lemon Beurre Blanc Sauce

GRILLED SOFT-SHELL CRABS

8 jumbo soft-shell crabs

⅓ cup olive oil

1 tablespoon kosher salt

1 tablespoon coarsely ground black pepper

2 teaspoons Blackening Seasoning (page 18)

STONE-GROUND GRIT CAKES

Makes 8 cakes

2 cups cooked stone-ground grits

½ cup all-purpose flour

1 teaspoon salt

1 teaspoon freshly ground black pepper

Peanut oil, for frying

LEMON BEURRE BLANC

Makes 1 cup

¼ cup freshly squeezed lemon juice

¼ cup white wine, preferably dry

2 tablespoons finely chopped shallots

⅓ cup heavy cream

½ pound (2 sticks) cold unsalted butter, cut into tablespoons

½ teaspoon kosher salt

¼ teaspoon finely ground black pepper

1 tablespoon finely minced fresh basil

Grilled lemon halves, arugula, and/or chives for garnish (optional)

continued

To make the crabs, start by cleaning them. (If you get precleaned crabs, you may omit this step.) For fresh crabs, clean them under running water. Fold back the sides to expose and remove the gills. Using kitchen shears, cut across the crab slightly behind the eyes and mouth and remove the small sac directly behind the mouth.

Preheat a grill to medium-high. Brush the crabs with the olive oil and season with the salt, pepper, and Blackening Seasoning. Place the crabs on the grill and cook for 8 to 10 minutes (depending on their size), turning every couple of minutes. The crabs should be orange and firm to the touch when done.

To make the grit cakes, spread the grits ¾ inch thick on a small sheet pan and cool. Using a large biscuit cutter, cut the cooled grits into circles (or just cut into squares with a knife). Pour the flour onto a plate, add the salt and pepper, and stir to combine. Gently remove the grit cakes from the sheet pan and dredge each in the flour mixture, coating all sides. Into a medium to large heavy skillet (cast iron works great here), pour the peanut oil to cover the bottom, roughly ¼ inch deep, and heat to

approximately 350°F. (Medium heat on your stovetop will be around this temperature.) Using a spatula, lay the grit cakes in the oil without crowding. Fry for 3 to 4 minutes, or until golden, then flip each cake over and repeat on the other side. Fry in batches if necessary.

To make the lemon beurre blanc, bring the lemon juice, wine, and shallots to a boil over medium-high heat. Continue to cook for 4 minutes, whisking occasionally, until the mixture reduces and thickens. Add the heavy cream and boil for 1 minute. Lower the heat to medium or medium-low and start adding the butter 1 to 2 tablespoons at a time, letting the butter almost melt before adding the next tablespoon or 2. (I know! I just want to chunk it all in there at once, too, but that ruins the sauce, so don't do that.) As soon as all the butter melts, season with salt and pepper, remove, and serve as this doesn't hold too long.

To serve, lay 2 grit cakes shingled on a plate, shingle 2 crabs over the grit cakes, and drizzle with Lemon Beurre Blanc. Garnish with a grilled lemon half and top with micro arugula or chives if desired.

We have always tried to vacation on the coast, and a deep-sea fishing trip is usually in order. Mahi-mahi is one of the most beautiful fish, with their amazing blues and greens and unique shape. My daughter, Lauren, has always been the lucky one on our trips and typically catches the largest fish of the day. One memorable trip to Key West landed us a bounty of mahi-mahi. We kept one fish and took it to a local restaurant to prepare, and it was absolutely delicious. Serve this on a bed of rice with some Bacon-Wrapped Asparagus with Pink Peppercorn Vinaigrette (page 138) and you will receive raves from the crew.

Serves 4

Grilled Mahi-Mahi with Meyer Lemon Butter

MEYER LEMON BUTTER

4 tablespoons (½ stick) salted butter, softened, preferably Homemade Butter (page 150)

¼ teaspoon salt

¼ teaspoon white pepper

¼ teaspoon granulated garlic

1 tablespoon fresh Meyer lemon (juice of ⅓ lemon)

MAHI-MAHI

1½ pounds mahi-mahi, cut into 6-ounce fillets

2 tablespoons olive oil, for brushing the fish

2 teaspoons Blackening Seasoning (page 18) or Southwest Spice Blend (page 17)

⅔ Meyer lemon, sliced, for garnish

To make the butter, in a small bowl stir all the ingredients until well incorporated. Place a small strip of plastic wrap on a counter. Place the butter on the plastic wrap and form it into a roll using the plastic wrap. Refrigerate the rolled butter for at least 1 hour before using.

Prepare a medium-hot grill, preferably with a light amount of fruitwood smoke. Lightly brush the fish with olive oil, then lightly season each fillet. (While I generally go with a blackening seasoning or my Southwest Spice Blend, mahi-mahi will do well seasoned with just about any blend you want.) Ensure your grill is fully heated up and grates are oiled, then place the fillets on the grill and cook for 4 to 5 minutes per side (up to 6 minutes, depending on thickness). The fish is done when it has firmed to the touch and is opaque. Remove from the grill and place each fillet on a plate. Unroll the plastic wrap and cut the butter into "coins." Lay a coin on each grilled mahi-mahi fillet after you have plated it. Garnish the fish with the lemon slices.

Scallops are a tricky item, and the quality really depends on where you get them. I will always pass on "wet" scallops that have been plumped with water and preservatives, making them impossible to sear. "Dry"-packed scallops are usually available only on the coast or via a good seafood purveyor and, as they have a shorter shelf life, are generally more expensive—but they are worth it. When you see a beautifully seared scallop in a restaurant, it is always going to be a dry-packed scallop. You can also purchase frozen scallops that have been handled properly; just read the ingredients carefully for "no added water."

I love the fresh zip the jalapeño brings to the bacon, which also makes an outstanding BLT.

Serves 4

Jalapeño Bacon-Wrapped Scallops with Blood Orange Glaze

JALAPEÑO BACON

10 slices bacon

1 cup syrup and jalapeños from Candied Jalapeños (page 47) or pickled jalapeños

½ fresh jalapeño chile, chopped

1 clove garlic, lightly crushed

SCALLOPS WITH BLOOD ORANGE GLAZE

20 jumbo scallops (1½ to 2 pounds total)

3 blood oranges

1 tablespoon olive oil

2 tablespoons honey

1 teaspoon red wine vinegar

1 teaspoon minced garlic

1 teaspoon minced fresh jalapeño

1 teaspoon bacon reserved grease

1 tablespoon Grillin' Shake (page 22)

To make the bacon, in a resealable plastic bag, mix the bacon with the candied jalapeños and syrup, fresh jalapeños, and the garlic. Seal and remove as much air as possible. Marinate for up to 12 hours, then use in recipes as regular bacon after lightly patting dry.

To make the scallops, on a griddle over medium-high heat, parcook the bacon until it has begun rendering fat but is not fully browned, then remove and cool, reserving the bacon grease and cutting each cooled bacon slice in half. Pat the scallops dry and wrap each one in a half bacon slice secured with a skewer, 5 scallops per skewer, then place the skewers in the fridge. Juice the blood oranges into a small saucepan and add the olive oil, honey, red wine vinegar, garlic, and minced jalapeño. Simmer for 5 minutes, until the sauce thickens and reduces slightly. Pour about 2 tablespoons into a small bowl for glazing the scallops and reserve the rest.

Remove the scallops from the fridge and lightly brush them with the reserved bacon grease, then very lightly season both sides with Grillin' Shake. Lay the skewers on an oiled grill over high heat and cook for about 2 minutes. Lightly glaze the scallops and cook them for another 2 minutes, then flip. After flipping, brush the cooked side with glaze and glaze them again after 2 minutes. Remove the scallops when they are slightly firm to the touch and opaque. Serve with Grilled Caesar Salad (page 39) or cooked rice and drizzle the remaining sauce over the plated scallops.

While this isn't a grilled recipe, it is normally done outside on a propane burner to keep the massive amounts of steam, laden with spices, from making everyone's eyes water for hours. While I have been known to consume some crawdads (crayfish or crawfish, for you folks outside the South), I'm more partial to the corn, potatoes, and sausage usually found cooking alongside the mini-crustaceans in the spicy broth. Crawdad season starts in the early spring, and roadside boiled crawfish stands spring up to let everyone know fresh crawdads are available. (Note: Shrimp can easily be substituted in a crawdad boil, but you will need to adjust the steeping time as the shrimp need only 4 to 7 minutes, depending on their size.)

For this recipe you will need a big stockpot (about 5 gallons for the following recipe) with a strainer, a cooler that you're not especially fond of, and a good propane burner. I am scaling this recipe down for entertaining just a few people, but most of the time in these parts, you'll find people talking about cooking sacks of crawdads (around 40 pounds). Allow around 1 pound of crawfish per person.

Serves 8

Southern Crawdad Boil

8 pounds live crawfish

4 lemons

½ pound (2 sticks) unsalted butter

4 to 5 bay leaves

1 cup Blackening Seasoning (page 18), plus ¼ cup for serving

¼ cup coriander seeds

2 tablespoons cayenne (optional)

2 pounds sausage links, preferably andouille, cut into 2 to 3-inch pieces

4 cloves garlic, lightly crushed

3 pounds small to medium red potatoes, rinsed

8 ears corn, shucked and cut in half

2 medium white onions, peeled and quartered

Place the crawfish in a cooler, fill with water, and drain. Repeat until the water runs clear. Sort through the crawfish and remove any dead ones.

Fill a 5-gallon stockpot half-full with water. Place the strainer in the pot. Cut the lemons in half and squeeze the juice into the pot, then drop the lemons in (discarding the seeds in the strainer) along with butter, bay leaves, Blackening Seasoning, coriander seeds, and cayenne, if using. Add the sausage, garlic, and potatoes to the pot and bring to a boil. Cook for 10 minutes, then add the corn and onions and bring back to a boil for 5 minutes, until the potatoes start to soften. Add the crawfish and cook for 1 more minute. Turn off the burner, cover the pot, and let everything sit in the water for 20 to 25 minutes, until the potatoes are fully soft. Carefully pull the strainer up, allowing the food to drain.

Traditionally at large boils, we line an outdoor table with several sheets of newspaper and dump the contents of the baskets directly on the table. People then mill around the table, enjoying the spicy bounty. For a few people, I would suggest dumping the contents back into a cooler (cleaned, and this time with the plug inserted), sprinkling it all with Blackening Seasoning, and letting people get what they wish with tongs.

MELISSA'S
TIP

A note from experience: Keep lots of trash cans around, as the shells tend to go everywhere when people start enjoying the crawfish, and you do NOT want to discover a crawfish shell in a couple of days. On a similar note, crawfish boils are best held the day before the garbage truck runs.

Shrimp are susceptible to overcooking, either by grilling or by using acidic marinades. This can be a good thing, as in the case of ceviche, or it can be a bad thing, as in the case of the flavorless, rubbery things you were served when you went over to your cousin Eddie's for his infamous shrimp boil. This marinade is flavorful and quickly flavors the shrimp—without overdoing it. While you're preparing the dish, cook a pot of white rice.

Serves 4

Spicy Agave Grilled Shrimp with Cool Cilantro Sauce

COOL CILANTRO SAUCE

Juice of 1 lime

2 tablespoons minced fresh cilantro

2 tablespoons minced fresh basil

1 teaspoon minced garlic

½ teaspoon grated peeled fresh ginger

½ teaspoon kosher salt

¼ teaspoon freshly ground black pepper

1 cup Greek yogurt

SPICY AGAVE GRILLED SHRIMP

1½ tablespoons olive oil

1 teaspoon minced garlic

2 tablespoons water

2 tablespoons agave syrup

2 canned chipotle chiles, minced, plus 2 teaspoons adobo sauce

1 tablespoon minced fresh cilantro

2 teaspoons tamarind paste

1½ pounds (2½ 5 count) shrimp, peeled and deveined, preferably Gulf shrimp

To make the sauce, whisk all the ingredients together in a small mixing bowl. Serve on the side as a dipping sauce for the shrimp.

To make the shrimp, in a large bowl, whisk together all the ingredients except the shrimp. Add the shrimp to the bowl and toss to cover with the marinade. Marinate the shrimp in the refrigerator for 15 to 20 minutes, then place on skewers, 8 to each skewer. Cook the shrimp skewers on a medium-hot grill, 3 to 4 minutes per side, until the shrimp is pink, opaque, and lightly firm to the touch. Remove the skewers from the grill and serve over cooked rice, with Cool Cilantro Sauce served on the side.

CHAPTER 8

STAR OF THE SHOW SIDES AND WHATNOT

Although I have included many of my recipes for sides earlier, with a main dish when I believed that side was integral to the dish, I've added more of my favorites here. In my world, entire meals are often made of "side items," and absolutely no one would complain about the absence of a meat course. Growing up, many of my meals consisted of nothing but pinto beans, turnip greens, and a nice slab of freshly made corn bread. Today, either in the restaurants or at a barbecue contest, I am constantly focused on cooking meats. After having your head inside a smoker day after day, sometimes you just crave a delicious "side" item (or two, or three!).

Biscuits are another item that makes a frequent appearance on any Southern table. My husband often tells me of his grandmother making biscuits by "feel" three times a day, and the large, wooden "biscuit" bowl that she kept her flour in and just added ingredients to, stirring in just enough flour to make the perfect biscuit. I have included some different biscuit recipes here, just to show that they can be quite versatile. Any of these items can be the "Star of the Show" on your next dinner table, whether or not there's a main course!

I love the light little pop you get from pink peppercorns and use them quite often when cooking at home. This dish takes a bit of preparation time to wrap the bacon around the asparagus but is worth it. Serve as appetizers or as a side, allowing 4 per person.

Serves 4

Bacon-Wrapped Asparagus with Pink Peppercorn Vinaigrette

PINK PEPPERCORN VINAIGRETTE

1 teaspoon minced shallot

1 teaspoon honey

1 teaspoon Dijon mustard

2 tablespoons white balsamic vinegar

½ teaspoon kosher salt

¼ cup extra virgin olive oil

1½ teaspoons pink peppercorns, lightly cracked with a mortar

BACON-WRAPPED ASPARAGUS

16 fresh asparagus spears, trimmed

8 slices thin-cut bacon, cut in half

1 teaspoon Basic "Memphis-Style" BBQ Rub (page 17)

To make the vinaigrette, in a small mixing bowl, whisk the shallots, honey, mustard, balsamic, and salt and whisk to combine. Slowly drizzle in the olive oil while whisking to emulsify. Whisk in the peppercorns. Allow the mixture to sit for 30 minutes for the flavors to combine, then lightly whisk again before serving.

To make the asparagus, wash and dry each spear, then wrap each one with a half-slice of bacon, using a toothpick on each end to secure. Place on a sheet pan when done, then lightly sprinkle them with the BBQ rub. On a medium-hot grill, place asparagus perpendicular to the grill grates and grill for 4 to 5 minutes per side, until the bacon is crispy. Place on plates and drizzle with the Pink Peppercorn Vinaigrette.

Arranged on a platter, this makes a beautiful side dish. I take care to get good grill marks on the vegetables to make them look appetizing and bring out the grilled flavor.

Serves 4 to 6

Summer Vegetable Medley

MARINADE

Makes almost ¾ cup

2 tablespoons honey

¼ cup olive oil

1 teaspoon diced fresh oregano

2 tablespoons diced fresh flat-leaf parsley

1 clove garlic, minced

2 tablespoons white balsamic vinegar

½ teaspoon coarsely ground black pepper

VEGETABLE MEDLEY

4 to 5 small carrots, carrot greens trimmed but left on, split in half lengthwise

1 medium sweet red onion, peeled and cut into wedges

1 bunch fresh asparagus, roots trimmed 1 inch from the base

1 red bell pepper

2 medium zucchini, cut into long strips

Smoked Sea Salt (page 28), for sprinkling

To make the marinade, whisk together all the ingredients. Put about half of the marinade in a resealable plastic bag along with the carrots, onion, asparagus, bell pepper, and zucchini. Seal the bag, pressing as much air out as possible, and shake to ensure the vegetables are coated. Marinate for 1 hour at room temperature or up to 6 hours in the refrigerator.

To make the vegetables, prepare a medium-hot grill. If your grates are large, a wire rack or grilling basket will help keep smaller pieces from sacrificing themselves to the fire gods. Grill the veggies for around 10 minutes, until tender and slightly charred. Remove the vegetables from the grill, place them in a serving bowl, drizzle the remaining marinade over them, and sprinkle lightly with Smoked Sea Salt.

I usually omit the mayonnaise part of this dish and just sprinkle the cotija cheese directly on the grilled corn, as I don't think fresh grilled corn really needs it—it's delicious without it. However, if you want to go traditional, the mayo is in the recipe.

Serves 4

Mexican Corn

2 tablespoons melted butter

1 tablespoon fresh lime juice

4 ears fresh corn, shucked and silks removed

1 teaspoon kosher salt

1 teaspoon coarsely ground black pepper

2 tablespoons mayonnaise (optional)

¼ cup grated cotija or Parmesan cheese

1½ teaspoons mild chili powder

¼ cup chopped fresh cilantro

In a small bowl, mix the melted butter and lime juice. Brush the mixture on the corn and lightly sprinkle it with salt and pepper.

Prepare a grill to cook on high heat. Grill the corn, turning every 2 or 3 minutes, until the corn is tender, 10 to 12 minutes. Remove the corn from the grill and let it cool slightly, then brush with the mayonnaise, if using. Place the cheese on a plate and roll the corn in it to coat, then sprinkle with chili powder and cilantro.

I will never tire of fresh summer corn, and I look for any way I can to prepare it. This can be done up to a day ahead of time for convenience.

Serves 4 to 6

Cool Corn Salad

6 ears fresh corn, shucked, silks removed

1 medium red bell pepper

1 medium green bell pepper

1 medium jalapeño chile

1 medium red onion, peeled and cut into wedges

¼ cup olive oil, plus more as needed

½ cup chopped fresh cilantro

1 tablespoon minced garlic

Juice of 2 limes

Salt and freshly ground black pepper

Prepare a grill to cook on high heat. Brush the corn, bell peppers, jalapeño, and onion with the olive oil and place on the grill. Grill the peppers until charred, then place in a paper bag or resealable plastic bag and seal. Cook the corn and onion until lightly charred and grill-marked, around 3 minutes per side for the corn, about 3 minutes per cut side for the onion. Remove and allow all items to cool. Remove the skin from the peppers, then stem, seed, and dice them and place them in a mixing bowl. Cut the kernels from the cob into the bowl. Dice the onion and add to the bowl, then mix in the cilantro, garlic, and lime juice and stir. Season with salt and pepper. Refrigerate for 1 hour before serving.

Pintos and turnip greens make a common appearance on my table, and I frequently cook more than needed. This recipe is a great use for any leftover pintos, and they work well with any Texas-tinged main dish.

Serves 4

Ranch Beans

4 slices bacon, chopped

½ cup diced red onion

1 cup diced tomato

1 tablespoon minced garlic

1 jalapeño chile, cored and diced

2 cups cooked pinto beans, with cooking liquid

2 tablespoons chopped fresh cilantro

Salt and freshly ground black pepper

In a medium stockpot, cook the bacon until crispy, then add the onion and cook for 3 minutes, until softened. Add the tomato, garlic, and jalapeño. Add the beans to the pot, stir, and simmer until hot. Stir in the cilantro, season with salt and pepper to taste, and serve.

Succotash is a very traditional side item, but I like to make mine a little on the wild side. It is wonderful during the peak of summer when the corn is just ripe and fresh butter beans (or small lima beans) are available. Grilling the corn brings out a little sweetness, plus it adds to the appearance of the dish.

Serves 4 to 6

Grilled Corn Succotash

5 to 6 ears corn, shucked and silks removed

1 tablespoon olive oil

4 slices bacon, chopped

½ cup diced white onion

1 tablespoon diced fresh jalapeño chile, seeds removed

1 tablespoon diced garlic

1 cup coarsely chopped fresh tomato

1 pint fresh butter beans (baby lima beans)

1 teaspoon salt

1 teaspoon freshly ground black pepper

Brush the corn with the olive oil and grill the ears on a medium-hot grill until you have grill marks on all sides, about 2 minutes per side. Remove the corn from the grill, cool, and slice the kernels from the cob.

In a medium stockpot over medium-high heat, fry the bacon until crisp. Remove with a slotted spoon and set aside. Add the onion, jalapeño, and garlic to the rendered fat and cook for 2 minutes, then add the tomato and cook for 2 to 3 more minutes. Add the butter beans and enough water to cover them. Lower the heat and simmer for 15 minutes, then add the corn and continue to simmer for 15 to 20 minutes, until the butter beans are tender. Season with salt and pepper, top with the bacon, and serve.

Brussels are one of my favorite sides. It's really amazing how a vegetable so universally hated by youth everywhere can suddenly become a favorite. I love to make sure to get some of the outer leaves a little charred as it adds to the texture and flavor.

Serves 4 to 6

Spiced Brussels Sprouts

2 tablespoons balsamic vinegar

2 tablespoons white balsamic vinegar

1 teaspoon agave syrup

2 teaspoons store-bought hot sauce or Roasted Pepper Hot Sauce (page 29)

1 teaspoon Dijon mustard

1 teaspoon minced garlic

½ teaspoon kosher salt

¼ teaspoon freshly ground black pepper

½ cup extra virgin olive oil

1 pound brussels sprouts, ends trimmed, cut in half

1 small white onion, peeled and cut into wedges

Smoked Sea Salt (page 28)

In a small bowl, whisk together the balsamic vinegars, agave, hot sauce, mustard, garlic, kosher salt, and pepper. While whisking, drizzle in the olive oil to form a quick emulsion. Place the brussels sprouts and onion in a pan, drizzle about half of the balsamic mixture over them, then turn the vegetables so the cut sides are down in the pan. Marinate for 20 to 30 minutes.

Prepare a medium-hot grill. Place the sprouts and onion in a grilling basket on the grill. Cook for 4 to 5 minutes, then flip over. Allow to cook for another 4 to 5 minutes, then move to a cooler part of the grill to cook for 10 to 15 minutes, until tender. Remove the grilling basket from the grill and empty it into a medium bowl, then drizzle the vegetables with the remaining balsamic and lightly sprinkle them with Smoked Sea Salt.

Hoppin' John garnished with Candied Jalapeños (page 47)

Hoppin' John is a traditional black-eyed pea dish, usually served over rice. Peas are very simple to cook and tend to absorb other flavors very well, providing a nice backdrop for the main meal. This is a pretty simple method and will simmer merrily along, getting nice and happy. Hoppin' John can also stand up as a main dish by itself if you're so inclined.

Serves 4 to 6

Hoppin' John

2 slices bacon, chopped

1 tablespoon peanut oil

½ cup diced red onion

¼ cup finely diced celery

¼ cup diced green bell pepper

1 tablespoon minced garlic

1 teaspoon minced jalapeño chile (optional)

1 bay leaf

1 teaspoon salt

½ teaspoon freshly ground black pepper

1 pound fresh black-eyed peas (or ½ pound dried, soaked overnight)

2 cups chicken stock

2 cups cooked white rice

Minced scallion, for garnish

In a medium stockpot, fry the bacon in the peanut oil fry for 3 to 4 minutes, until browned. Add the onion, celery, bell pepper, garlic, and jalapeño, if using, and cook until the onion turns translucent, about 5 minutes. Add the bay leaf, salt, and pepper and stir, then add the black-eyed peas and cover with stock. Bring to a boil, then decrease the heat and simmer for 30 minutes, stirring occasionally. Check for tenderness, and if needed continue to cook for 10 to 15 minutes more. (Fresh peas typically cook more quickly than dried/soaked peas, so watch for this. Dried peas will also typically absorb more of the stock, and you may have to add water.) The finished consistency should be thick without being mushy. Cook the rice while the black-eyed peas are simmering.

To serve, lay down a bed of rice, then top with the peas. Garnish with the scallion and serve.

Making butter with a food processer almost seems like cheating! This recipe is so versatile you can make flavored butters for basically anything, either by adding the flavors in while spinning or by mixing them in with part of the finished product. For those of you who wish to do everything the traditional way, you obviously haven't churned butter by hand before.

Makes 1 pound

Homemade Butter

1 quart heavy cream

2 teaspoons kosher salt

Pour the cream into the food processor and add the salt. Turn the processor on and let it run. After about 5 minutes, the cream will have whipped, and you might be tempted to taste it. Don't do that as it does not taste like whipped cream should! Instead, leave the processor alone to keep doing its thing, about 10 more minutes. You'll think, "This isn't working!" But then, just when you've about given up, the whipped cream will just disintegrate and break into liquid and solids. Let it spin for another minute, then turn the processor off. Pour the contents through a fine-mesh sieve over another container; the solids are butter, and the liquids are buttermilk. (Save the buttermilk for use in Mini Sage Biscuits with Sage Butter, page 154.) Press the butter between your hands to remove as much liquid as possible and transfer the butter to a bowl. Press the butter in the bowl with a fork and pour off any liquid that accumulates. To keep, I form it into a cylinder using clear plastic wrap and store in the fridge for up to 1 week.

Corn bread is an important part of many Southern meals, and my trusty cast-iron skillet has been put to good use making it. When I have guests, I like to make corn muffins, and this recipe is always a hit.

Both my husband and I have fond memories as children of going and watching someone press sugarcane and cook down the sap into sorghum molasses. Generally this was accomplished with a mule connected to a log, which turned the grinder as the mule walked around and around while someone fed sugarcane into the mechanism. (It was a much simpler time, and there weren't as many channels on TV, so you did what you could for entertainment.) I still enjoy molasses, and my Molasses Butter is the perfect contrast (and complement) to the Corn Muffins.

Makes 12 muffins

Corn Muffins with Molasses Butter

5 tablespoons unsalted butter

½ cup diced yellow onion

¼ cup seeded diced jalapeño

1½ tablespoons minced garlic

4 eggs

1⅔ cups self-rising yellow cornmeal

1 cup all-purpose flour

1⅓ cups buttermilk

¼ cup sugar

¼ cup finely diced red bell pepper

2 ears corn, shucked, silks removed, and kernels cut off cobs

3 teaspoons kosher salt

MOLASSES BUTTER

8 tablespoons (1 stick) butter (preferably Homemade Butter, page 150), at room temperature

2 tablespoons molasses

Preheat the oven to 400°F and spray a 12-cup muffin pan with nonstick spray. (I prefer coconut oil spray.) In a small skillet, melt the butter over medium heat, then add the onion and jalapeño. Cook for 2 minutes, then add the garlic and cook until the onion is soft and the garlic is golden.

In a large mixing bowl, crack and lightly whisk the eggs, then place the remainder of the ingredients, including the sautéed items, in the bowl and stir to incorporate. Using a spoon, fill each muffin cup about three-quarters full. Place the muffin pan in the oven and bake for 15 minutes, or until a toothpick inserted in the middle comes out clean. Remove the pan from the oven and set aside to cool for 5 to 10 minutes, then remove the muffins from the pan.

To make the butter, in a small bowl, mix the butter and molasses together to incorporate. You can add these to a mixer (it's best to double the recipe if you do so to give it volume for the mixer) and blend on medium-high speed for 3 to 4 minutes to make a whipped molasses butter. Will keep refrigerated for 1 week.

Sweet potatoes are a constant companion for the Southern cook. You name the dish and we'll figure out a way to work a sweet potato into it. Sweet potatoes have been a mainstay in the South as they love to grown in our climate and soil, and they last for a long time when stored properly. Sweet potatoes, usually "cured" in a root cellar, provide sweet deliciousness all through the year. For this I like to bake instead of boiling the sweet potatoes to help pull moisture out of them.

Makes 12 to 15 biscuits

Sweet Potato Biscuits

1¼ cups all-purpose flour, sifted, plus ¼ cup for rolling

½ teaspoon salt

3 tablespoons sugar

½ teaspoon ground cinnamon

1 tablespoon plus 1 teaspoon baking powder

1 cup cooked, mashed sweet potato (preferably baked)

6 tablespoons unsalted butter (¾ stick), at room temperature, divided

2 to 3 tablespoons buttermilk

1 teaspoon flaked sea salt

Cornmeal, for sprinkling on pizza stone

Preheat a Big Green Egg or a dry grill (no water pan) to 450°F, with a pizza stone inserted. In a large bowl, place the flour, salt, sugar, cinnamon, and baking powder. In another large bowl, mix the sweet potato and 4 tablespoons of the butter together using a fork, then add and cut the sweet potato mixture into the flour until it makes a coarse dough. Add 2 tablespoons of the buttermilk and keep mixing. If the dough looks too dry or flaky, add 1 more tablespoon of buttermilk, until the dough holds together and all of the flour is incorporated. Turn the dough onto a floured cutting board, roll it out to a ½-inch thickness, and cut it with a 2¼-inch biscuit cutter. (Like a speed limit, this size is merely a suggestion.) Melt the remaining 2 tablespoons butter. Brush the tops of the biscuits with the melted butter and lightly sprinkle flaked salt on top. Lightly sprinkle cornmeal on the pizza stone, then place the biscuits on it and bake for 10 to 12 minutes, until the biscuits have risen and are lightly crusted.

MELISSA'S
TIP

Most breads can be made in a grill setting as long as you can keep even temperatures. Set up the grill for indirect cooking and use a baking stone over the lower-heat area. Generally, I like the crispier bottoms you get from using the stone, but if you prefer, just set a lightly oiled baking pan holding the bread on top of the stone, as you would in your oven. I normally let any wood cook down to the coals before I bake breads on the grill as they can very quickly pick up the smoke flavor. But, if you like it, add fresh wood and enjoy!

Sage is my favorite herb, to the point that my family makes fun of me because of my sage addiction. One time, I decided to cut down on my sage usage, but then the moment passed, and I got over it. The end. These are great served with Smoked Chicken and Wild Rice Soup (page 112).

Makes about 15 small biscuits

Mini Sage Biscuits with Sage Butter

2 cups all-purpose flour, plus more for kneading

1 tablespoon baking powder

¼ teaspoon baking soda

1 tablespoon minced fresh sage

¾ teaspoon salt

⅓ cup cold butter, plus 1 tablespoon melted butter, divided

¾ cup buttermilk

Flaked sea salt, for sprinkling

SAGE BUTTER

¼ cup Homemade Butter (page 150)

1 teaspoon minced fresh sage

Kosher salt

Preheat a grill (preferably a ceramic grill like the Big Green Egg) to 450°F, using the indirect method and a baking stone.

In a large mixing bowl, stir together the flour, baking powder, baking soda, sage, and salt until well blended. Using a fork, cut the ⅓ cup of cold butter into the flour. (It should look like coarse crumbs when fully mixed.) Make a well in the middle and add the buttermilk, then stir until the flour is incorporated. Lightly flour a cutting board, transfer the dough from the bowl to the board, and lightly knead the dough until it looks almost smooth. Roll out the dough to a ½-inch thickness. Using a 1½-inch biscuit cutter, cut the biscuits out and put them on a greased baking sheet (or directly on the baking stone for a slightly crispier bottom). Place the baking sheet on the baking stone on the grill for 10 to 12 minutes, until the biscuits are golden brown, then remove and brush the biscuit tops with the remaining 1 tablespoon melted butter and lightly sprinkle with sea salt.

To make the butter, mix the butter and sage together in a small bowl. Taste and season with salt if needed. Will keep, refrigerated, for 1 week.

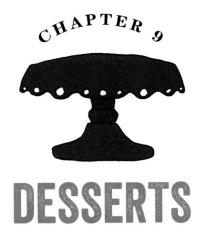

CHAPTER 9

DESSERTS

I really like pie. I don't think desserts have to be over-the-top sweet, nor do they have to be hugely complicated to make. While I certainly appreciate and am in awe of some of the edible arts my pastry chef friends are capable of producing, the beautiful simplicity of a well-made pie is just as artful to me. Did I mention I really like pie?

In this chapter I have some desserts prepared on the grill as well as more traditional cooking mediums. Cooking desserts such as pies or even cakes is pretty straightforward on any grill where you can generate indirect heat and maintain a certain temperature. Flour-based items, such as a cake, tend to pick up smoke flavor very quickly, so when making a cake I use very light smoke and ensure my fire is burning very cleanly. Fruit, on the other hand, generally benefits from a direct flame and higher heat and smoke levels. Peaches and pineapples are especially forgiving on the grill, and caramelizing the fruit helps bring out the sweetness while adding a texture contrast.

I have fallen in love with Meyer lemons, so much so that I have two trees on my back porch. While they don't bear enough fruit for my addiction, every once in a while I get to make a pie using the fruit from my own trees. It somehow tastes just a little bit better. As an aside, if smelling a Meyer lemon bloom is not on your bucket list, it should be!

Makes one (9-inch) pie, serving 8

Meyer Lemon Chess Pie

PIE CRUST (OR SUBSTITUTE A 9-INCH STORE-BOUGHT ONE)

1¼ cups all-purpose flour

8 tablespoons (1 stick) cold unsalted butter, cut into pieces

¼ teaspoon salt

5 tablespoons ice water

FILLING

1½ cups sugar

1 teaspoon grated Meyer lemon zest

¾ cup freshly squeezed Meyer lemon juice, about 3 lemons

8 tablespoons (1 stick) unsalted butter, melted

1½ tablespoons cornstarch

1 tablespoon yellow cornmeal

¼ teaspoon salt

4 large eggs, lightly whisked

To make the pie crust dough, combine the flour, butter, and salt in a bowl with a fork, breaking up the butter until it is BB pellet–sized. Sprinkle the water, 1 tablespoon at a time, over the dough and stir until all the flour is moistened. Shape into a ball, cover with plastic wrap, and refrigerate for 30 minutes to an hour.

When ready to bake the pie crust, preheat the oven to 425°F, remove the dough from the fridge, and roll into a 12-inch circle. Lay it over a 9-inch pie pan (not deep dish). Press down and crimp the edges around the pan, then indent with a fork to give the crust texture. Place aluminum foil over the top of the dough and use pie weights to keep the bottom flat. Bake for 15 minutes, remove from the oven, and carefully remove the pie weights and foil (they're hot!). Return to the oven for 5 more minutes, until the pie crust is golden brown. Cool completely before adding filling.

To prepare the filling, preheat the oven to 350°F. In a mixing bowl, whisk together the sugar, zest, lemon juice, melted butter, cornstarch, cornmeal, and salt. Pour in the eggs and whisk until thoroughly blended. Pour into the baked pie crust and bake for 50 to 55 minutes, until the center is set. Use a pie shield or aluminum foil to cover the edges of the pie crust if it starts turning too brown. Remove from the oven and place on a cooling rack to cool.

This makes a refreshing end to any summertime meal and is super simple. Grilling and smoking fruit is one of my favorite things to do and is a welcome contrast to a meat-centric meal. Most fruits pick up smoke flavor quickly, so it takes only a few minutes to get some grill marks and smoke flavor. Grill this before you cook your entrée and then put in the fridge to let the flavors meld and provide a cooling treat after dinner. This fruit selection is one of my favorites, but just about any seasonal fruit can be used.

Serves 4 to 6

Grilled Fruit Salad

1 whole fresh pineapple, peeled, cored, and cut into rings

1 Fuji apple, cored and sliced into wedges

2 peaches, peeled, pitted, and cut into wedges

1 teaspoon olive oil

1 teaspoon fresh lemon juice

1 cup seedless green grapes, sliced in half

1½ tablespoons honey

½ teaspoon red wine vinegar

4 or 5 fresh basil leaves, cut into slivers

Prepare a medium grill. Place the pineapple, apple, and peaches in a mixing bowl with the olive oil and lemon juice. Toss gently to coat all the fruit with the oil. Place the fruit on the grill to cook until it begins to caramelize, about 3 minutes. Then flip and cook for an additional 2 minutes. Pull the fruit from the grill and cut into about 1-inch pieces. Place in a serving bowl with the grapes, add the honey and vinegar, and stir. Top with the basil slivers and place in the fridge for at least 30 minutes before serving. Stir again right before serving.

This has become one of my favorite desserts and is easy to prepare on a grill or in the oven. It's not too sweet, but has a nice light flavor that hits the spot after a great meal. Clafoutis is a very easygoing dessert and will work with just about any type of fruit, but one of my favorites is caramelized fresh figs. I have to buy mine at the grocery store because the dang squirrels keep eating them before they get ripe. Next cookbook will include smoked squirrel.

Serves 8

Caramelized Fig Clafoutis

FIGS

3 tablespoons butter

2 tablespoons light brown sugar

15 Black Mission figs, stemmed and sliced lengthwise

CLAFOUTIS

1 cup half-and-half

½ cup granulated sugar, plus more for the pan

2 large eggs

2 teaspoons vanilla extract

Finely grated zest of ⅓ lemon

¼ teaspoon salt

¼ cup plus 2 tablespoons all-purpose flour

1 tablespoon melted butter, for the pan

Confectioners' sugar, for dusting (optional)

To prepare the figs, in a nonstick skillet over medium-high heat, melt the butter and add the brown sugar, stirring until dissolved. Place the figs cut-side down in the pan, adding only as many as will fit in a single layer. Cook for 1 to 2 minutes, until the figs are golden brown. Remove the figs from the pan and set aside. Caramelize the second batch of figs if necessary.

Set up a grill for 2-zone cooking at 425°F with a pizza stone over the higher-heat side. Combine the half-and-half, ½ cup granulated sugar, eggs, vanilla, lemon zest, and salt in a blender. Pulse for 10 seconds, until the ingredients are incorporated. Add one-third of the flour and pulse again for 10 seconds. Repeat with the remaining flour, then allow to stand for 30 minutes. Using a 10-inch cast-iron skillet, brush the bottom with melted butter and dust with granulated sugar. Pulse the batter again, then pour into the skillet. Place the figs in the batter, cut-side up.

Place the skillet on the pizza stone and bake for 15 minutes, then move the skillet to the lower-heat side and vent the grill to lower the temperature to 325°F. Cook for approximately 20 minutes, until the top of the custard is golden brown. Let cool before serving.

Every summer I keep a small herb garden on my porch, and the difference in these herbs versus store-bought is amazing. Basil is one of the hardier ones, and a little water and some sunlight is about all it takes to have a basil "green thumb." This simple dish brings together two of my favorite summertime flavors and is quite simple to make. I love this because I can make the shortcake and whipped cream ahead of time and grill the strawberries just after I start the grill and before I cook my entrée. Dessert is done! You can easily substitute store-bought shortcake or pound cake here, and it will be good—but not *as* good.

Serves 8

Grilled Strawberry Shortcake with Basil Whipped Cream

SHORTCAKE

2¼ cups all-purpose flour

1 tablespoon plus 1 teaspoon baking powder

2 tablespoons granulated sugar

¼ teaspoon salt

⅓ cup solid white vegetable shortening

1 egg, lightly beaten

⅔ cup milk

GRILLED STRAWBERRIES

2 pints fresh strawberries, stemmed and cut in half

1 cup granulated sugar

5 to 6 leaves fresh basil, chopped

BASIL WHIPPED CREAM

2 cups heavy cream

¼ teaspoon vanilla extract

2 tablespoons confectioners' sugar

½ cup packed fresh basil leaves, minced

2 or 3 fresh basil leaves, slivered, for garnish

To prepare the shortcake, preheat the oven to 425°F and grease a 9-inch square baking pan. In a bowl, stir the flour, baking powder, sugar, and salt together to incorporate. Cut in the shortening until crumblike. Add the egg and milk and stir until combined. Pour into the prepared pan and bake for 13 to 15 minutes, until golden. Let cool, cut in half (making 2 layers), then cut into 9 portions (8 for serving and one for testing!).

Grill the "top" pieces of shortcake to achieve grill marks, about 2 minutes per side on an oiled hot grill.

To prepare the strawberries, place the strawberries in a grilling basket with a handle. Place the basket on a hot charcoal grill, preferably, or on a hot gas grill with a smoke box using wood chips. Cook for about 2 to 3 minutes per side, trying to get the berries some heat and smoke but not overcook them. Remove the basket, pour the strawberries into a bowl, and spread the sugar and basil over them. Place in the freezer for 15 minutes, stir, then put in the refrigerator for at least 30 minutes.

To prepare the whipped cream, in a stand mixer fitted with the whisk attachment, mix the cream, vanilla, and confectioners' sugar. Mix on medium-high speed until soft peaks form. Gently fold in the minced basil. Place the whipped cream in the refrigerator until ready to serve.

To serve, place a piece of ungrilled shortcake on each plate and spoon the strawberries over it. Shingle on a grilled piece of shortcake, top with a generous dollop of basil whipped cream, and garnish with slivered basil.

This makes a deceptively easy dessert that is sure to impress anyone. It is a no-bake cheesecake, so have room in the fridge for it to set up and firm. For a crisp, defined top layer, pour the ganache over the cheesecake while it's still in the form. If you prefer a drizzled look, loosen the form and then pour in.

Serves 10 to 12

Peanut Butter Cheesecake with Chocolate Ganache

12 tablespoons (1½ sticks) unsalted butter, softened, divided

2 cups plus 2 tablespoons graham cracker crumbs, divided

½ cup granulated sugar

1 pound cream cheese, softened

2 cups peanut butter

2 cups confectioners' sugar

1 tablespoon vanilla extract

1 cup heavy cream

CHOCOLATE GANACHE

8 ounces semisweet chocolate chips

2 cups heavy cream

Preheat the oven to 350°F. Using 2 tablespoons of the butter, grease the sides (not bottom) of an 8-inch springform pan, then sprinkle 2 tablespoons of the graham cracker crumbs on the sides.

Melt the remaining 10 tablespoons butter and mix with the remaining 2 cups of graham cracker crumbs and the granulated sugar. Place in the bottom of the pan and press to form a crust. Bake for 8 minutes, then let cool. In a large bowl, blend the cream cheese and peanut butter until smooth. Add the confectioners' sugar and vanilla and blend until mixed. Whip the 1 cup heavy cream until stiff peaks form and fold into the peanut butter mixture. Pour into the springform pan and level the top using a spatula.

To make the ganache, in a double boiler combine the chocolate and 2 cups cream over low heat. Stir until the chocolate is melted and the mixture has thickened. Remove from the heat and let cool for 2 to 3 minutes while stirring, then pour over the top of the cheesecake.

Refrigerate for at least 4 hours to allow it to set. Remove the sides of the springform pan before serving. Use a sharp knife run under warm water to slice.

This is the way my mother has made cobbler since I can remember. It is super easy and produces a light, cakelike "crust" over the peaches. I like to give it a grilled twist by grilling the peaches and then cooking it on the grill. The subtle flavor goes through the peaches, and the hint of smoke catches in the crust to really make this taste of summertime.

Serves 6 to 8

Grilled Peach Cobbler

1 tablespoon butter, melted

5 peaches, cut in half and pitted

3 cups water

⅛ teaspoon salt

2 cups sugar, divided

1 cup self-rising flour

¾ cup milk

Set up a grill for indirect heat to cook at 350°F. Lightly butter the cut side of the peaches, then place them, cut-side down, on the hot side of the grill. Cook for 4 to 5 minutes, until the peaches begin to soften and have nice grill marks. Remove the peaches, cool for a minute, then peel and cut into 1-inch cubes.

In a medium Dutch oven over the high-heat side of the grill, mix the water, peaches, salt, and 1 cup of the sugar and cook for 1 hour, until the peaches are soft and the syrup is thickened, stirring occasionally and ensuring the peach mixture doesn't burn.

In a mixing bowl, mix together the remaining 1 cup of sugar, the flour, and the milk to make a thin batter. Pour into the center of the peach mixture and allow it to spread. Move the Dutch oven to the low-heat side of the grill, uncovered, and cook for 30 minutes more, until the top is golden and the batter is set. Remove and let cool, then spoon out portions into bowls (being miserly with them will reward you with more to enjoy later!).

Pie is always a good thing, and when you have fresh blueberries, it can be a great thing. Even though this doesn't have a lot of butter (what's ¼ cup between friends), the texture in the pie and the light crust that develops are so delicious and buttery that I just call it a butter pie. This is my husband's favorite pie—it's not overly sweet but just right. In this recipe I'm just calling for a premade pie crust, but you are welcome to make your own—although that means you will be 20 to 30 minutes farther away from having a slice of this. The topping is optional as the pie is good by itself.

Serves 6 to 8

Blueberry Butter Pie with Blueberry Sauce

BLUEBERRY SAUCE

Makes 1½ cups

2 cups blueberries

2 cups sugar

1½ cups water

BLUEBERRY BUTTER PIE

1 cup fresh blueberries

1 (8-inch) deep-dish pie crust

4 tablespoons (½ stick) unsalted butter, softened

½ cup buttermilk

3 large eggs

½ teaspoon vanilla extract

2 cups sugar

½ cup all-purpose flour

Pinch of salt

To make the sauce, in a small saucepan, bring all the ingredients to a boil over medium-high heat. Decrease the heat to medium and cook at a low boil for 1 hour to reduce until syrupy and thick. Turn off the heat and let cool down some before serving. Will keep for 3 days—if it lasts that long!

To make the pie, lay the blueberries on top of the crust and set aside. Preheat the oven to 350°F.

Using a mixer, beat the butter, buttermilk, eggs, and vanilla in a mixing bowl at low-medium speed until the butter is cut into small pieces, about 1 minute.

In a separate bowl, whisk the sugar, flour, and salt together before adding to the mixing bowl. Blend for 30 seconds, until incorporated. Pour into the pie crust and bake for 55 to 60 minutes, until set. Check on the pie after 40 minutes and cover lightly with foil if the crust is browning too much. Drizzle a tablespoon of warm sauce on each slice to serve.

Most people have that one special person that they are close to in their family. My person was my grandfather. We would hang out under a shade tree, rebuilding car transmissions, hook the wagon up to the horses and go for rides, hang out at the local coffee shop (which also served as the local BBQ joint after breakfast), basically spending time together where he would impart common sense and wisdom to his granddaughter. He was a man of few words, so when he spoke, I was tuned in and listening, eager to absorb the next morsel of information. "I really like a good coconut cake," he would say. I didn't want to hear that; I wanted to hear more war stories, more engine rebuilding knowledge, the common sense to know when peanuts are ready to be pulled from the ground. He did love coconut cake, so this one is for my grandfather.

This recipe picks up just a hint of smoke from cooking on the grill to give it that special touch.

Serves 10 to 12

Coconut Cake

1 coconut

¾ cup solid white vegetable shortening

1 cup sugar, divided

4 medium eggs, separated, yolks whisked

½ teaspoon vanilla extract

2¼ cups cake flour

2¼ teaspoons baking powder

½ teaspoon salt

ICING

1 cup sugar

⅓ cup water

⅓ teaspoon cream of tartar

2 egg whites

1½ teaspoons vanilla extract

Set up a grill for indirect heat to cook at 350°F, with a baking stone. It is very important that you monitor the temperature level of the baking stone. Grease 2 (9-inch) round cake pans.

Drain the liquid from the coconut and reserve. Remove the husk and, using a potato peeler, shave 1 cup of coconut meat. Grate the rest using a box grater.

In a stand mixer, cream the shortening and ½ cup of the sugar. Add the whisked egg yolks and vanilla and mix for 1 minute. Mix in ¾ cup of the grated coconut.

In a separate bowl, sift the cake flour, baking powder, and salt. Add a quarter of this mixture at a time, alternating with pouring in some of the ¾ cup coconut liquid from the coconut. (If you didn't get enough from the coconut, add coconut milk from a can or regular milk to make up the difference.) Mix until the wet and dry ingredients are completely integrated into the batter.

In a separate bowl, beat the egg whites until stiff peaks form, then gradually whisk in the remaining ½ cup of sugar and fold into the batter using a spatula. Pour the batter into the prepared cake pans, place on the baking stone on the grill, and bake for 35 to 40 minutes, until the cakes have risen and a toothpick inserted in the center comes out clean. Place on a wire rack to cool.

continued

Raise the grill temperature to 400°F, place the 1 cup coconut shavings in a pie pan, taking care not to break them up, and place on the grill for 5 minutes (keep an eye on them), until the shavings are browned and toasty.

To prepare the icing, boil the sugar, water, and cream of tartar in a small saucepan until it reaches 242°F on a candy thermometer. Cover and remove from the heat. Beat the egg whites on medium-high speed until very

stiff peaks form, then slowly pour the hot syrup into the egg whites while still blending. Add the vanilla and blend until smooth.

To assemble, place 1 cake layer on a cake plate and ice, then sprinkle some grated smoked coconut on top of the cake. Add the second layer of cake and cover with icing. Then place the toasted shaved coconut all around and on top of the cake. The cake will keep for 3 to 4 days.

Acknowledgments

I am graced with a 300-person barbecue family, the employees of Memphis Barbecue Company. Thanks to my team at our restaurants for covering for me when I have been working on this book. A heartfelt thanks goes to Marissa Roberts and Donnavun Thomas for helping me test recipes. All these employees of Memphis Barbecue Company are what make the restaurants so wonderful. When you love your job, you never work a day in your life!

Thanks to Evan Carl for dropping everything and helping me. I can always depend on you!

A big thanks to Ray Lampe and the people at Big Green Egg for getting me outfitted in a hurry.

Thanks to Richard Gilbert for making me look so much better than I deserve.

I am always grateful that my grandmother, Tracy Pounders, helped me understand some of my childhood memories and answered my questions at odd hours. Also, thanks for being my friend. I love you to the moon and back!

A big thanks to my mom, Beverly Weaver, for being my official taste tester and for carting off copious amounts of food from my house while I was testing the recipes in this book.

My official sous-chef on this project was my daughter, Lauren Cookston. Thank you for all your hard work. You are a very special person, and my advice to you is: Don't follow in my footsteps, create your own footprint on the world!

This book would not have been possible without my husband, Pete. He hates all the mushy stuff, so I'll just say that he has definitely qualified for sainthood after putting up with me for all these years. I've nicknamed him "my other three-quarters."

Doneness Chart for Beef and Pork

125°F . . . Rare
135°F . . . Medium rare
145°F . . . Medium
150°F . . . Medium done
160°F . . . Well done

Pickled Grilled Onions (page 47)

Metric Conversions and Equivalents

METRIC CONVERSION FORMULAS

To Convert	Multiply
Ounces to grams	Ounces by 28.35
Pounds to kilograms	Pounds by 0.454
Teaspoons to milliliters	Teaspoons by 4.93
Tablespoons to milliliters	Tablespoons by 14.79
Fluid ounces to milliliters	Fluid ounces by 29.57
Cups to milliliters	Cups by 236.59
Cups to liters	Cups by 0.236
Pints to liters	Pints by 0.473
Quarts to liters	Quarts by 0.946
Gallons to liters	Gallons by 3.785
Inches to centimeters	Inches by 2.54

COMMON INGREDIENTS AND THEIR APPROXIMATE EQUIVALENTS

1 cup uncooked rice = 225 grams
1 cup all-purpose flour = 140 grams
1 stick butter (4 ounces · ½ cup · 8 tablespoons) = 110 grams
1 cup butter (8 ounces · 2 sticks · 16 tablespoons) = 220 grams
1 cup brown sugar, firmly packed = 225 grams
1 cup granulated sugar = 200 grams

OVEN TEMPERATURES

To convert Fahrenheit to Celsius, subtract 32 from Fahrenheit, multiply the result by 5, then divide by 9.

Description	Fahrenheit	Celsius	British Gas Mark
Very cool	200°	95°	0
Very cool	225°	110°	¼
Very cool	250°	120°	½
Cool	275°	135°	1
Cool	300°	150°	2
Warm	325°	165°	3
Moderate	350°	175°	4
Moderately hot	375°	190°	5
Fairly hot	400°	200°	6
Hot	425°	220°	7
Very hot	450°	230°	8
Very hot	475°	245°	9

APPROXIMATE METRIC EQUIVALENTS

Volume

¼ teaspoon	1 milliliter
½ teaspoon	2.5 milliliters
¾ teaspoon	4 milliliters
1 teaspoon	5 milliliters
1¼ teaspoons	6 milliliters
1½ teaspoons	7.5 milliliters
1¾ teaspoons	8.5 milliliters
2 teaspoons	10 milliliters
1 tablespoon (½ fluid ounce)	15 milliliters
2 tablespoons (1 fluid ounce)	30 milliliters
¼ cup	60 milliliters
⅓ cup	80 milliliters
½ cup (4 fluid ounces)	120 milliliters
⅔ cup	160 milliliters
¾ cup	180 milliliters
1 cup (8 fluid ounces)	240 milliliters
1¼ cups	300 milliliters
1½ cups (12 fluid ounces)	360 milliliters
1⅔ cups	400 milliliters
2 cups (1 pint)	460 milliliters
3 cups	700 milliliters
4 cups (1 quart)	0.95 liter
1 quart plus ¼ cup	1 liter
4 quarts (1 gallon)	3.8 liters

Weight

¼ ounce	7 grams
½ ounce	14 grams
¾ ounce	21 grams
1 ounce	28 grams
1¼ ounces	35 grams
1½ ounces	42.5 grams
1⅔ ounces	45 grams
2 ounces	57 grams
3 ounces	85 grams
4 ounces (¼ pound)	113 grams
5 ounces	142 grams
6 ounces	170 grams
7 ounces	198 grams
8 ounces (½ pound)	227 grams
16 ounces (1 pound)	454 grams
35.25 ounces (2.2 pounds)	1 kilogram

Length

⅛ inch	3 millimeters
¼ inch	6 millimeters
½ inch	1.25 centimeters
1 inch	2.5 centimeters
2 inches	5 centimeters
2½ inches	6 centimeters
4 inches	10 centimeters
5 inches	13 centimeters
6 inches	15.25 centimeters
12 inches (1 foot)	30 centimeters

Information compiled from a variety of sources, including *Recipes into Type* by Joan Whitman and Dolores Simon (Newton, MA: Biscuit Books, 1993); *The New Food Lover's Companion* by Sharon Tyler Herbst (Hauppauge, NY: Barron's, 2013); and *Rosemary Brown's Big Kitchen Instruction Book* (Kansas City, MO: Andrews McMeel, 1998).

INDEX

Andrews McMeel Publishing
a division of Andrews McMeel Universal
1130 Walnut Street, Kansas City, Missouri 64106

www.andrewsmcmeel.com

www.yazoosdeltaq.com

16 17 18 19 20 SHO 10 9 8 7 6 5 4 3 2 1

ISBN: 978-1-4494-7809-4

Library of Congress Control Number: 2015952441

Editor: Jean Z. Lucas
Art Director: Holly Ogden
Creative Director: Tim Lynch
Photographer: Stephanie Mullins
Food Sylist: Teresa Blackburn
Production Editor: Maureen Sullivan
Production Manager: Carol Coe
Demand Planner: Sue Eikos

ATTENTION: SCHOOLS AND BUSINESSES
Andrews McMeel books are available at quantity discounts
with bulk purchase for educational, business, or sales
promotional use. For information, please e-mail the
Andrews McMeel Publishing Special Sales Department:
specialsales@amuniversal.com.